FORENSIC ANTHROPOLOGY

SOLVING CRIMES WITH SCIENCE:
Forensics

FORENSIC ANTHROPOLOGY

Angela Libal

Mason Crest

Mason Crest
450 Parkway Drive, Suite D
Broomall, PA 19008
www.masoncrest.com

Printed and bound in the United States of America.

First printing
9 8 7 6 5 4 3 2 1

Series ISBN: 978-1-4222-2861-6
ISBN: 978-1-4222-2869-2
ebook ISBN: 978-1-4222-8955-6

The Library of Congress has cataloged the
hardcopy format(s) as follows:

Library of Congress Cataloging-in-Publication Data

Libal, Angela.
  Forensic anthropology / Angela Libal.
    p. cm. — (Solving crimes with science, forensics)
  Audience: 012.
  Audience: Grades 7 to 8.
  Includes bibliographical references and index.
  ISBN 978-1-4222-2869-2 (hardcover) — ISBN 978-1-4222-2861-6 (series) — ISBN 978-1-4222-8955-6 (ebook)
  1. Forensic anthropology—Juvenile literature. 2. Victims of crimes—Identification—Juvenile literature. 3. Criminal investigation—Juvenile literature. 4. Forensic sciences—Juvenile literature. I. Title.
  GN69.8.L532 2014
  614.17—dc23
                                2013006959

Produced by Vestal Creative Services.
www.vestalcreative.com

Contents

Introduction

By Jay A. Siegel, Ph.D.
Director, Forensic and Investigative Sciences Program
Indiana University, Purdue University, Indianapolis

It seems like every day the news brings forth another story about crime in the United States. Although the crime rate has been slowly decreasing over the past few years (due perhaps in part to the aging of the population), crime continues to be a very serious problem. Increasingly, the stories we read that involve crimes also mention the role that forensic science plays in solving serious crimes. Sensational crimes provide real examples of the power of forensic science. In recent years there has been an explosion of books, movies, and TV shows devoted to forensic science and crime investigation. The wondrously successful *CSI* TV shows have spawned a major increase in awareness of and interest in forensic science as a tool for solving crimes. *CSI* even has its own syndrome: the "*CSI* Effect," wherein jurors in real cases expect to hear testimony about science such as fingerprints, DNA, and blood spatter because they saw it on TV.

The unprecedented rise in the public's interest in forensic science has fueled demands by students and parents for more educational programs that teach the applications of science to crime. This started in colleges and universities but has filtered down to high schools and middle schools. Even elementary school students now learn how science is used in the criminal justice system. Most educators agree that this developing interest in forensic science is a good thing. It has provided an excellent opportunity to teach students science—and they have fun learning it! Forensic science is an ideal vehicle for teaching science for several reasons. It is truly multidisciplinary; practically every field of science has forensic applications. Successful forensic scientists must be good problem solvers and critical thinkers. These are critical skills that all students need to develop.

In all of this rush to implement forensic science courses in secondary schools throughout North America, the development of grade-appropriate resources that help guide students and teachers is seriously lacking. This new series: *Solving Crimes With Science: Forensics* is important and timely. Each book in the series contains a concise, age-appropriate discussion of one or more areas of forensic science.

Students are never too young to begin to learn the principles and applications of science. Forensic science provides an interesting and informative way to introduce scientific concepts in a way that grabs and holds the students' attention. *Solving Crimes With Science: Forensics* promises to be an important resource in teaching forensic science to students twelve to eighteen years old.

1

WHAT IS FORENSIC ANTHROPOLOGY?

For thirty years she was a legend with no name. Known only as "Tent Girl," the young woman's body was found in May of 1968, wrapped in a tarp in the forest near Eagle Creek, Kentucky. She had been left to die of suffocation. By the time her body was found, it was decomposed beyond recognition. The **medical examiner** guessed she was a teenager. Her only known features were a height of approximately 5'1"; a weight of 110 to 115 pounds (50 to 52 kilograms); and short, reddish-brown hair. A forensic artist used her autopsy photos to make sketches of what she probably looked like in life. No match was found. Tent Girl was buried in Georgetown Cemetery, near the place of her murder. Her story inspired compassion in townspeople, and a monument was made for her, engraved with the forensic artist's portrait. Tent Girl quickly became a local legend.

Twenty years later, the daughter of the man who discovered Tent Girl began dating Todd Matthews, her future husband. Matthews became enthralled with Tent Girl's story and was determined to find her identity. For the next ten years he searched for a name to go with the face. He found her one night while he was cruising Internet websites devoted to descriptions of missing persons. Her name was Barbara Ann ("Bobbie") Hackmann Taylor. Based on her sister's description, authorities were convinced that the body should be exhumed. A forensic anthropological analysis of the bones showed that she was actually around age twenty-five. Her bones also showed that she was a Caucasian female, and she had given birth to at least two children. This matched her sister's description of a woman born in 1943, 5'2" with reddish-brown hair, who had left two children behind.

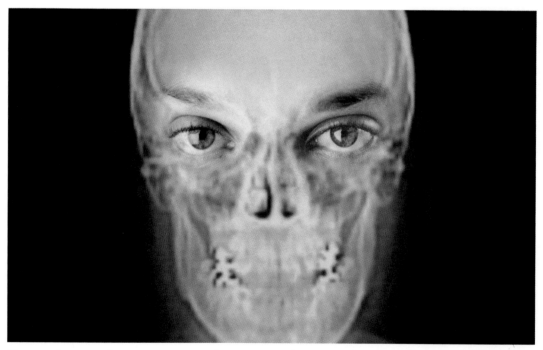

Forensic examiners may superimpose a photograph over the picture of a skull to help identify a victim.

The sister provided a photograph of Bobbie. Forensic examiners superimposed this photograph over a picture of her skull. It appeared to be a match. To be sure, dental records were ordered because now they had a possible name. Finally, a DNA test was done on the bone tissue and the blood of Bobbie's surviving relatives. It was a match. Thirty years after her murder, Barbara Ann was given a name, and although her killer was never brought to justice, her family finally had the peace of at least knowing what had become of her.

Defining Forensic Anthropology

Forensics is the science of crime investigation. *Anthropology* is the study of human beings. Within the science of anthropology, there are three main disciplines: cultural anthropology, the study of human societies; physical anthropology, the study of the physical evolution and structure of humankind; and archaeology, the study of human artifacts.

Forensic anthropology is a branch of physical anthropology. It is based on osteology, or the study of bones. Forensic anthropologists use their knowledge of the human skeleton and of criminal investigation to identify the victims of violent crimes and mass disasters. Their efforts can help determine the victims' manners of death, return the remains of loved ones to their families, and identify killers.

Forensic anthropologists work with law enforcement personnel in cases where human remains cannot be easily recognized by sight. These are cases where the body has decomposed, become skeletonized, or mummified. When a body is fresh, the forensic pathologist's job is to determine identity and manner of death. When the soft tissues (skin, muscles, internal organs) have been removed or destroyed, the forensic anthropologist steps in.

Questions for the Dead

Every study of a set of remains begins with questions the forensic anthropologist must answer:

Are the bones human?
How old was the person at the time of death?
Was the person female or male?
What was the person's ethnic background?
What was the person's stature?
What unique, individual characteristics did the person have?
What was the manner of death?

Answering "Are the bones human?" determines if there will be a criminal investigation, or archaeological study in the case of ancient remains, or if suspicions can be laid to rest. If the answer to this question is yes, the forensic anthropologist must do her best to answer the next four questions, sometimes called the "Big Four": age, sex, race, and stature. After these are known, the last two questions, unique characteristics and manner of death, can be investigated. Hopefully, the answers to these questions will bring an identification of the victim and justice in the case of violent crimes.

Recognizing Human Bones

Physical anthropologists study the human skeleton in great detail. They are trained to recognize human bones, even when the bones are *disarticu-*

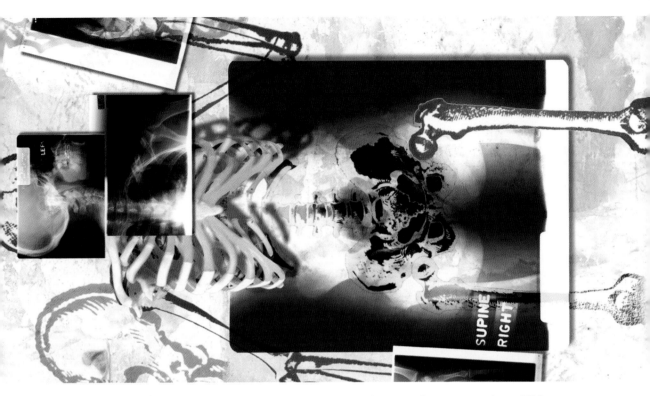

Forensic anthropologists must reconstruct skeletons from remains. This requires skill and in-depth knowledge of the human skeletal structure.

lated or fragmented. A trained forensic anthropologist can recognize even tiny bits of bone and body parts, whether they are from a human or another type of animal, and what body part they once were.

Once a set of bones is determined to be human, the forensic anthropologist must reconstruct the skeleton. The bones are laid out in anatomical order, from the top of the skull to the bones of the feet. To do this, the anthropologist must know what each bone in the human body looks like and where it goes. This may seem easy if the bone is a whole skull or large piece of pelvis—but this task becomes more challenging when the bones are small or broken into pieces. The ability to tell left-side bones from right-

What Is Forensic Anthropology?   **13**

Explosions and other disasters can cause bodies to be torn and spread over large areas.

side bones is only the beginning of the problem. A forensic anthropologist must be able to look at a piece of bone and know from which bone it came and how to piece that bone back together.

Cracking the Case

When human remains are found, law enforcement officials are required to determine whose they were and from where they came. Human remains might be found in an unexpected location for several reasons. People occasionally stumble across burial sites of Native or ancient peoples. Sometimes ancient remains of an accident or crime victim have been found thousands of years after the person's death, as in the case of Ötzi, the Iceman. Wartime sites—where battles were fought or where genocide was committed—have yielded mass graves and acres of scattered bones.

Mass disasters oftentimes require the identification of human remains in various stages of intactness. Transit disasters, like airplane and train crashes; natural disasters, such as floods and earthquakes; and terrorist attacks can cause bodies to be torn into many small pieces and scattered over a wide area.

Forensic anthropologists are most often consulted in cases involving violent crime. When a set of remains is found that is not an ancient artifact or the result of a known war or disaster, a criminal investigation must take place. Investigators must determine whether the victim died of natural causes or at the hands of another person. When the remains are of the victim of a violent crime, investigators must do their best to identify not only the victim but also the killer.

Forensics' Birth

The first known book on forensic science, *The Washing Away of Wrongs*, was written by Tz'u Sung and published in China in 1247 CE. The book describes many aspects and techniques of forensic investigation, including the stages of decomposition of bodies and the use of flies to find invisible blood residue on weapons.

2

IDENTIFYING THE VICTIM

All that remained of Louisa Leutgert's bones could have fit into a tablespoon. When she disappeared in 1897, her husband, Adolph Louis Leutgert, was known as the sausage baron of Chicago. Neighbors became suspicious of Leutgert's story that his wife was visiting relatives when his two young children began asking door-to-door for information about where their mother had gone. A search of Leutgert's five-story sausage factory and its grounds turned up four small pieces of bone, a false tooth, a hairpin, a burned corset stay, and an earring with the engraved initials "L.L."

Adolph Leutgert was brought to trial for the murder of his wife. However, the jury was unable to reach a verdict based on the evidence and the lack of remains. For the first time in history, an anthropologist was called to testify in court.

The anthropologist was George Dorsey. By examining the bones, he could tell they were a human metacarpal bone from a hand, the end of a rib, one piece of toe bone called the phalanx, and another from the joint of a big toe. Dorsey's measurements showed that the bones had come from a young woman. The corset piece, hairpin, and earring showed that woman was Louisa Leutgert. Her husband had boiled her body with 375 pounds (170 kilograms) of potash and 50 pounds (23 kilograms) of arsenic in a vat in his sausage factory, reducing all but those four tiny bone fragments to a pile of jelly within two hours. This substance was found staining the floor beneath the vat. Adolph Leutgert was convicted of murder and sentenced to life in prison, and the science of forensic anthropology was born.

Louisa's case shows how forensic anthropologists can deduce the identity of a person and her manner of death from even the smallest fragments of bone. To do this, forensic anthropologists must use their knowledge of human bones to answer the four key questions discussed in the last chapter.

How Old Was the Victim?

Several parts of the skeleton give clues to age:

- the sutures of the skull
- teeth
- the ends of the clavicle (the collar bone)
- the ends of the long bones in the arms and legs
- the pubic symphysis (the area where the hip bones meet)
- the joints between bones, where bones and cartilage meet

The adult human body contains 206 bones, but babies begin life with around 300 separate bones. Cartilage connects the bones to each other,

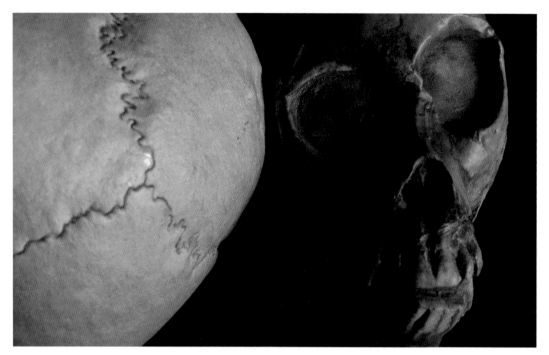

The bones of the skull are joined by cranial sutures.

making up the skeleton. As a person grows, the cartilage changes to bone, fusing many of the body's bones to one another. This process is called ossification. Ossification begins at birth and happens in a predictable pattern. After bones ossify, aging breaks them down again. Since this pattern is known and is nearly the same for all people, a forensic anthropologist can study the ossification and aging of a decedent's bones and determine the age at the time of death.

The soft spot on a baby's head is one of the most visible places where ossification is seen. The bones of the skull are separate in a newborn and grow together along immovable joints called cranial sutures. These sutures close gradually over a person's lifetime, only becoming fully fused after the age of forty.

Identifying the Victim   **19**

Age can be estimated from the ends of the long bones, because these bones do not begin as single pieces. They are made up of a long shaft, called the diaphysis, and end bones, called the epiphyses. As the bones grow and ossify, the epiphyses and diaphyses grow together. By the age of fourteen, the **humerus** has ossified at the elbow. By age twenty, it has ossified at the shoulder. The femur has ossified at the thigh by the age of seventeen and at the knee by the age of eighteen.

The clavicle is another place where the age of an individual can be determined. It begins as two bones, slowly fusing together at the center of the chest by the time a person is between twenty-four and thirty years old.

Certain bones in the rest of the body also ossify gradually. The bones of the hands and feet usually have ossified by the age of fifteen, ankle bones by the age of sixteen, and wrist bones by the age of nineteen.

A forensic anthropologist will examine a skeleton's joints to help determine its age.

The pubic symphysis helps tell a person's age because it wears down over a lifetime. The ends of the bones start off looking bumpy. The bumps smooth out during a person's twenties and thirties, and then become rough again as the bone wears down around the age of forty.

Joints help tell a person's age because they break down as they grow older. This breakdown is called osteoarthritic lipping and happens as the cartilage gets thinner due to wear and tear. The edges of the bones begin to grow over this thin cartilage in bumpy, jagged formations. A person in his seventies could be expected to have quite a lot of osteoarthritic lipping, while someone in her twenties usually would not.

Like bones, teeth grow in a predictable pattern. A **forensic odontologist** or dentist can study the teeth or jaws of the remains and tell if the person was a child, teenager, or adult. In the case of children and teenagers, the odontologist can tell the age by the **deciduous teeth** that have grown in or been lost, and which permanent teeth have erupted through the gums. Human **dentition** has thirty-two teeth: three molars, two premolars, one canine tooth, and two incisors on each side of the jaw. A child usually has his first permanent incisors (two front teeth) and first molars by the age of seven, second incisors by eight, first premolars by ten, canines by eleven, second premolars and second molars by twelve, and third molars (wisdom teeth) by age twenty-five. If a person's third molars have erupted, the odontologist knows that person was an adult at the time of death; but since all the teeth have already grown in, he won't be able to tell the person's exact age from the types of teeth.

When anthropologists have small pieces of bone without joints, bone ends, or teeth, they can estimate age using the Kerley method. This technique takes a very thin slice of bone and places it under a microscope. With a microscope, the scientist can see the osteons, tiny passageways that once carried blood through the bone. These small passageways develop

Identifying the Victim   **21**

rings over time, much like the rings that can be seen in the trunk of a tree (only much smaller). Using a mathematical formula, age can be found by counting the number of rings and broken osteons compared to whole, un-marked osteons. Since this method is difficult and damages the bones, it is only used as a last resort or in extraordinary circumstances.

Is the Victim Male or Female?

Sex is also told by measuring certain bones. The pelvis and the skull are the easiest and most accurate bones to determine sex. People often think of the pelvis and skull as each being a single bone, but the pelvis is made up of seven different bones and the skull has twenty-nine bones. The skeletons of boy and girl children are the same and cannot be told apart until they begin to change at **puberty**.

As a girl matures into a woman, her pelvic bones spread and her hips become much wider than a man's. The female pelvis becomes wide and shallow, and if the anthropologist looks at it from above, she will see the pelvic inlet—a large, oval opening where the two sides join. Male pelvises remain narrow and deep, and their opening is heart-shaped. The notch at the bottom of each hip bone or ilium, where the sciatic nerve passes, is called the greater sciatic notch. This can also show a person's sex. In men, the angle of this notch is narrow, less than fifty degrees. In women, the angle of this notch is wide, over fifty degrees.

The area called the pubic symphysis is a piece of cartilage where the hip bones join in front. This softens, and the two sides of the pelvis sepa-rate if the woman gives birth to a child. After a baby's birth, this cartilage hardens again. A mark is left after this has happened twice. If this mark is seen, a forensic anthropologist will know that a woman has had at least two children.

While girls in puberty are getting wider hips, boys' skulls are changing. The skulls of men become more **robust** than the **gracile** skulls of women. In other words, women's skulls have rounded foreheads and chins with smooth bone above the eye sockets, while male skulls have foreheads that slope backward, squarer chins, and ridges of bone in the area of the eyebrows. The jawbones of males are squarer than those of females, and the mastoid process—the area where the jaw muscles attach—is larger. Men also have an occipital protuberance or a noticeable lump of bone at the bottom of the back of the skull.

If the pelvis and skull are missing, forensic anthropologists can make an educated guess about the sex of the decedent by measuring other bones

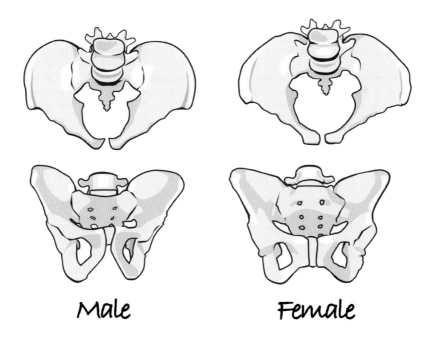

Male   Female

The pelvis can help a forensic anthropologist determine whether a decedent is male or female.

Jawbones Around the World

Sometimes a person has a trait that links her strongly to her ancestors, such as the shape of a jawbone. Australian Aboriginal and Polynesian Native people sometimes have a rounded chin bone. A trait called the Hapsburg jaw is carried by some Europeans. This means that the chin projects very far forward. A trait called rocker jaw is common among Native Hawaiians. This trait shows the jawbone is so rounded that it will rock back and forth on a flat surface.

and comparing them to known skeletons. Since men's shoulders are usually broader than women's, a long collarbone might show that a person was male. Many women are smaller than many men, so small bones might be judged to be female, while bones with large ridges where muscles were once attached might be assumed to be male. Good guesses can be made based on averages. However, there are plenty of tall, sturdy, and muscular women and small men with delicate builds, so the only way to be sure about the sex of a skeleton is to see the pelvis and the skull.

All people are unique, and everyone has individual traits. Many skeletons are intermediate, meaning that they have both female and male traits. In these cases, mathematical formulas are used to determine the ratio of male-to-female traits. Another complication is that some people, called transgender or transsexual people, were born as one sex but live as the opposite one. This can complicate identification of remains, since a skeleton might lead investigators to look for a person of one sex when all of the victim's acquaintances knew the person as another. This is something that forensic investigators often have to consider. Although transsexual people represent a small percentage of the population, they are disproportionately the victims of violent crimes.

What Was the Victim's Race?

Race can be a very sensitive topic. The word can call to mind a rainbow of skin and eye colors, hair textures, cultures, and parts of the world. To a physical anthropologist, though, race is a set of characteristics that skeletons have based on ancestry—and for an anthropologist, there are only three races: Negroid, Mongoloid, and Caucasoid. A skeleton can have a mixture of characteristics from two or even all three races—just like living people can inherit countless combinations of skin, hair and eye colors, and other physical features from their ancestors. Finding which racial features are most obvious helps an investigator narrow a search for a missing person.

Negroid includes people of African descent; Mongoloid of Asian, Native North and South American/First Nations, and Inuit descent; and Caucasoid of European descent. Race can be told by the shape of the skull and teeth and some of the body's joints.

Negroid skulls are more rounded than Caucasoid and Mongoloid skulls, with a longer **cranium**; a wide, smooth **nasal aperture**; and wide-set **ocular orbits**. Many Negroid skulls show prognathism, which is when the bone around the upper teeth projects forward. Also, the upper part of the molars is more textured. More than Mongoloid or Caucasoid skeletons, Negroid skeletons have a wider space between the bones that form the knee joint. Negroid bones are also usually heavier and denser.

Mongoloid skulls have a wide, flat face with prominent cheekbones, and a wide, flat nasal opening. The cranium is rounded. The incisors are often square and flat in the front, with a "shovel-shape" or U-shaped edges in the back. Only some Mongoloid skulls have teeth line up in what is called an edge-to-edge bite. This means that when the mouth is closed, the teeth of the upper and lower jaws line up with their edges touching.

Caucasoid skulls are angular and elongated, with a flatter back than Negroid skulls. Instead of being prognathic, they are orthognathic, which

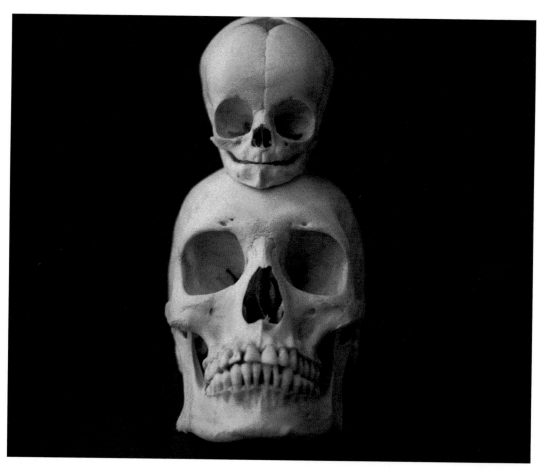

Differences in skulls help forensic anthropologists determine decedents' age, sex, and race.

means that the bones between the bottom of the nose and the chin are flat. Many Caucasoid skulls have a nasal spine, which is a spike of bone at the bottom center of the nasal opening. The nasal opening is usually tall and narrow, and the ocular orbits closer together than in other skulls. The chin often projects further forward. The incisors are more curved than Mongoloid incisors, and the tops of the molars are smoother than Negroid ones.

How Tall Was the Victim?

Along with age, sex, and race, knowing someone's height helps investigators identify a deceased person. Simply measuring the length of a skeleton is not enough to judge height. There is cartilage and flesh between a living person's bones, and it varies by sex, race, and age, as well as by the individual. The most common way to estimate height is by measuring a long bone, and then using a mathematical formula that takes into account the victim's age, sex, and race.

Most human bodies are proportionate. This means that if the length of one body part is known, lengths of other body parts can be calculated based on how many of the first part would "fit" into the second. For example, the length of the hand is approximately one-tenth of a person's height. If the length of the hand is eight inches (20 centimeters), multiplying it by ten will give the person's approximate height of eighty inches (200 centimeters).

Unfortunately for investigators, there is no accurate way to tell a person's weight from her skeleton. The amount of adipocere can point to the amount of body fat, as can grease-fire residue from around a burned body. If the areas where the muscles attached to the bone are well developed, an investigator will know that the person was muscular. It is also usually possible

Case Study: The Case of the Missing Leg

On April 19, 1995, the Murrah Federal Building in Oklahoma City, Oklahoma, was bombed in a terrorist attack. Timothy McVeigh and Terry Nichols detonated a truck bomb outside of the building, killing 168 people, many of them children attending a day-care center. Although McVeigh and Nichols went to trial as the sole perpetrators of the crime, some of the evidence pointed to a third person behind the bombing. When defense attorneys discovered an unaccounted-for leg among the remains found in the rubble, they were convinced that this was a piece of the missing bomber—a piece that could solve the puzzle and help the defense's case.

The leg, amputated just above the knee, was dressed in the remains of military fatigues, dark socks, and a combat boot. Could it be the leg of a terrorist in militia garb? Plastic shards from the bomb seemed to show its owner had been near the center of the blast. The leg was assumed to be a man's because of its dress and the fact it was unshaven, with dark, curly hair. The skin appeared light but was in a state of advanced decomposition.

The FBI called in a forensic anthropologist to study the leg. The notch of the knee joint showed that its owner was black. Investigation showed that the leg belonged to a woman. Even further investigation identified her as Airman First Class Lakesha Levy, a twenty-one-year-old member of the U.S. Air Force, killed while applying for a Social Security card and buried with the wrong leg. This second "wrong leg" turned out to belong to a white female—and investigators have still not found a third bomber.

to tell if a person was right- or left-handed from these muscle attachments, which can help in identification.

Individual Characteristics

After the forensic anthropologist has determined the victim's age, sex, race, and stature, she searches the skeleton for individual characteristics that might help her find the person's identity. These may be unusual traits the person was born with or changes in the skeleton caused by life events.

Many experiences can leave marks on the bones. Periods of malnourishment during childhood and adolescence, broken bones, muscular activity, habitual movements, or a sedentary lifestyle all leave traces. If the remains of a child show many periods where bones stopped growing, investigators will look for a child who was neglected, abused, or very poor. A healed fracture in the ankle may mean that a victim walked with a limp. Large muscle attachment areas on one side of the body might point to a person who had a job that required a lot of lifting, like a construction worker. Smooth muscle attachments could be someone with little physical activity. Daily habits can show up in bone, too. For example, people from cultures where it is common to sit in a chair when at rest have hip joints that develop differently from those who usually squat.

Each detail found in the skeleton is important. By studying a victim's bones, the forensic anthropologist hopes to discover the person's identity, give at least some sense of closure to loved ones, and bring justice to the killer.

3

GIVING FACES
TO THE LOST

To match remains with an identity, investigators must match the skeleton with records of a missing person. This is easiest if the person has been reported missing. A missing person's loved ones may file reports with several agencies. The largest databases of missing persons in the United States are the FBI's National Crime Information Center (NCIC), the National Center for Missing and Exploited Children, and the Nation's Missing Children's Organization and Center for Missing Adults (NMCO). In Canada, the largest databases are the Canadian Police Information Center (CPIC) and the Royal Canadian Mounted Police Missing Children's Registry (MCR). The Internet is an important place for information of all kinds, including international missing-persons databases.

These centers and databanks keep records of hundreds of thousands of children and adults who have been reported missing. However, just reporting someone missing does not mean his remains can be identified when found. First, the sheer numbers of reports can make it difficult to find the right identity. Second, the information recorded about the missing person might not be the information investigators need to identify remains. The forensic anthropologist needs information that will help identify bones. He will need to ask: Did the person have a skeletal disease or abnormality like scoliosis or arthritis? Did she ever suffer from a broken bone? What was the condition of his teeth? Even in the case of intact bodies, information that might seem trivial can be important. Did the missing person have jewelry she always

Missing person poster

wore? Scars? Tattoos or piercings? A special shape of fingernail or color of nail polish? Did he shave various parts of his body? If the person is female, has she given birth? If so, how many times? Even the smallest detail can identify a person—or let the right identification be overlooked.

The biggest problem with missing persons databases is that a person might never be reported missing. This can happen for a variety of reasons. Maybe the person was visiting from another country. Perhaps he had no family and few friends. She may have been murdered by a family member who did not report her disappearance. Maybe his loved ones simply did not know to whom to report the disappearance, or they were ashamed to admit that a loved one disappeared. Perhaps the report never made it from the police department into a national database, or the investigators may have stopped searching for an identity.

The most difficult cases for forensic scientists are unidentified remains. In these cases, the forensic anthropologist needs to reconstruct the victim's appearance and last moments from his bones, and find someone who will recognize and identify him.

Matching a Decedent to a Missing Person

If the decedent's teeth have been found and the person has ever had dental work, forensic investigators can find the person's identity through dental records. Once the investigators know the decedent's age, sex, race, and stature, they can begin searching for missing persons who fit that description. When they have possible matches, they can request dental records for those people and see if any fit the dental work of the remains.

Case Study: Finding Mwivano

Two young boys found the first bag on a warm summer day at a park near the Wisconsin River. Thinking they were looking at a dead animal, they called their mother. Immediately certain of what she was looking at, she quickly called the police. The decomposing remains in the bag were of a young woman.

Over the next few days, seven more bags were found. All contained various body parts of the same woman. Her body had been cut into pieces, with the skin of the face removed. From the soft tissue on the remains, the forensic pathologist determined that she had been a young, healthy, dark-skinned female. Fingerprint experts and other investigators worked hard on the case. No match could be found for the decedent's prints. With no tattoos, scars, or broken bones, there were very few hints to her identity. Since her teeth were perfect, there were probably no dental records. Without a face, investigators had no clue who she may have been.

Desperate for a name before the killer could disappear or strike again, the investigators called Dr. Emily Craig, a forensic anthropologist and forensic artist working in the state of Tennessee, and asked her to do a facial reconstruction.

Since the skull contained crucial evidence—the marks of the knife the murderer had used to cut off the victim's face—a copy of the skull was made with computer scans and lasers. Using this copy, the pathologist's report, and her own skill, experience at facial reconstruction, and extensive knowledge of human anatomy, Dr. Craig carefully built a face over the skull, trying to make a life-like image of the victim.

The skull had several confusing anomalies that made determining race difficult. Although Dr. Craig felt that some features were quite different from those of an African American, she ended up with a sculptural portrait of a young, black woman. Now the key was to put a picture of this sculpture in a place where it would be found by someone who would recognize the victim. That place turned out to be a bulletin board in a grocery store several towns away.

The victim was Mwivano Mwambashi Kupaza, a twenty-five-year-old student from Tanzania. This explained her non-American features but African skull. The woman who identified her was her cousin's former wife. The murderer was Mwivano's cousin, Peter Kupaza, a forty-year-old Wisconsin man. Young Mwivano, in a strange country with few acquaintances, had nowhere to go to get help after she was raped by her cousin. Shortly afterward, Kupaza murdered Mwivano, butchered the body, stuffed the body into plastic bags, and dumped the body into the Wisconsin River. Until Mwivano's body was identified, her Tanzanian relatives believed she was still living in the United States, while her Wisconsin acquaintances were told she had gone back to Tanzania.

After the identification, Mwivano's parents and other Tanzanian relatives where notified and came to the United States for Peter Kupaza's trial. Kupaza was found guilty and sentenced to life with no chance of parole for thirty years.

Another way to look for identity is through medical records, especially X-rays. The forensic anthropologist looks for identifying marks on the bones, such as healed breaks, fractures, surgical marks, amputations, bone diseases and abnormalities, and arthritis. Again, a list of possible matches is found and medical records are requested. If the records are of the victim, these changes in the bones should match the victim's X-rays.

Investigators also look for surgical appliances such as pacemakers, artificial hips, false teeth, and metal plates and pins. By their appearance or serial number, these appliances can be traced to doctors and manufacturers. If a manufacturer can be found, forensic investigators can find the doctor who installed the device and identify the patient who received it.

Investigators will compare skeletal remains to existing X-rays to help identify a victim.

Identifying a person is much easier if there is a list of possible identities from which to choose. In this way, missing person reports help investigators. These reports lead investigators to possible dental records and X-rays that may belong to the decedent.

The skull gives investigators the best chance to identify a decedent. The bones of the skull influence our appearance strongly. Two ways the skull is used to identify a person are photo superimposition and facial reconstruction. Photo superimposition is a technique that can be used to find the true identity from among a list of possible identities. The forensic anthropologist takes a photograph of the skull and a photograph of the person from life. A photograph showing the person's full face and looking forward is the best to use for this. The photograph of the person's face is superimposed over the photograph of the person's skull. If the skull belongs to the person in the picture, all points of the face will match. If a part of the face does not match the skull, then the skull does not belong to the person in the picture.

All these techniques are used when the investigators have some ideas about who the victim may have been. In cases in which there has been no missing-person reports filed, they need to give a face to the dead, hoping that someone who recognizes her will step forward and give the investigators a name.

Facial Reconstruction

Facial reconstruction is sometimes called facial approximation or facial restoration. It is a technique combining art and science. The forensic artist (usually also a forensic anthropologist) uses the skull and knowledge of human anatomy to sculpt a face that will look enough like the victim to be recognizable to someone who knew her. If the reconstruction is successful, someone who recognizes the victim will contact the investigators and give them the person's name. After they have a name, they can use other techniques, like dental records, X-ray matching, DNA testing, and photo superimposition, to confirm the identity.

The Russian Method and the American Method are two means of facial reconstruction. In both types, the forensic artist models a face onto the victim's skull or onto a cast of the skull. The difference is that the Russian Method builds models of each of the face's muscles before adding the "skin," while the American Method adds strips of clay to build the face without sculpting the muscles underneath.

To model on the skull, the bones must first be cleaned. This means that all remaining soft tissue must be gently removed by slowly boiling the bones in soapy water. After the bones are clean and dry, the artist either prepares the skull or makes a cast. A cast is very useful because it keeps the actual skull from being damaged.

A cast of the skull can be made by placing the skull in alginate—a rubbery substance that you're familiar with if you've ever had an impression of your teeth made at the dentist's office. After the alginate has hardened, the skull is removed, and the impression left in the alginate is filled with plaster or a special type of plastic. This plaster or plastic skull becomes the base over which the forensic artist sculpts the face.

Using computers and lasers is another way of making a model skull. This method is called rapid prototyping. It is accurate and especially useful if the investigators wish not to disturb the head in any way. A special X-ray-like picture called a CT-scan is taken of the head. The CT-scan can tell the difference between bone, soft tissue, cartilage, and teeth. This scan saves a detailed picture of the skull bones onto a computer. The computer uses guided laser beams to create an exact, three-dimensional model of the skull out of layers of plastic or of paper covered in **polyurethane resin**.

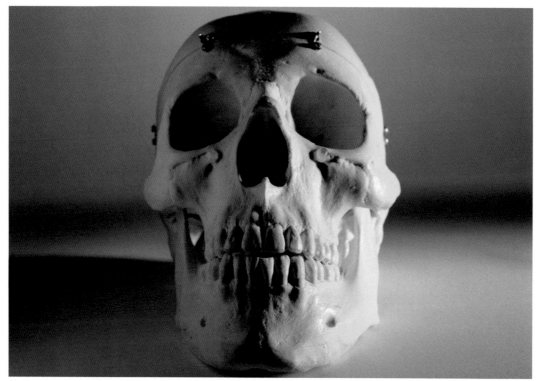

A forensic artist places pegs on the skull to indicate flesh thickness and uses these pegs to help sculpt the face.

After the forensic artist has a clean skull or model skull, she begins to build the face. First, the artist cuts tiny rubber or wooden pegs and gently glues them onto the head. These pegs show thickness of flesh at different points of the face. The artist uses a chart based on the victim's age, sex, and race to find averages for flesh thickness. Depending on the method the artist is trained in and the chart being used, between twenty-one and thirty-six different pegs will be glued onto the form.

The artist guesses eye color based on common types for the victim's racial group and region, and places glass eyes in the sockets. Then she begins to add the flesh by layering clay strips of different thicknesses onto the skull.

Case Study: Using Forensic Anthropology to Identify a Murderer

Back in November 1971, John List murdered his entire family. Police had no doubts about who had done the crime, since List left behind several notes explaining why he had to "free his family's souls." But List had disappeared.

Frank Bender, a forensic anthropologist, was hired by America's Most Wanted to create a bust showing how John List would look now. Although Bender had experience in aging faces, he realized he needed a psychological portrait, not just a physical one. A psychological profile would help him estimate how List might have altered his appearance, as well as how List's personality could influence the natural aging process. So Bender turned to criminal psychologist Richard Walter.

Together, psychologist and artist concentrated on specific behaviors:

- What would List's diet be?
- Would he still be around the same weight?
- What was his level of vanity?
- What was his degree of rigidity?
- How would he dress?
- What would his usual expressions be?

They looked over what was known of List's past habits and what others who had known him reported. Then they decided which of his traits would remain consistent, despite attempts to adopt a new identity. They figured List would be paunchier, with drooping skin around the jowls, deep worry lines, and a receding hairline. Despite the fact that List had a pronounced surgical scar behind his right ear that could betray him, he would not have opted for cosmetic surgery. He would likely still have financial difficulties and would be wearing glasses picked for a specific reason.

Finally, the bust was finished and taken to the television studio. The show was broadcast, and the forensic sculpture had its intended effect. A former neighbor of a man named Bob Clark called in with compelling details.

Ten days after the call, agents entered the office where Clark worked—about 240 miles (386 kilometers) from the original crime scene—and arrested him. Although he insisted they had made a mistake, his fingerprints confirmed his identity as that of John List. He was convicted of five counts of first-degree murder and sentenced to life in prison.

The most challenging part of sculpting the face is making the features resemble the person in life. These features include the lips, nose, eyelids, and ears. The artist does not know what the unidentified person really looked like, so the artist has to judge what the person probably looked like based on the smallest details of the skull and on averages for the victim's age, race, and sex. A facial reconstruction rarely looks exactly like the ac-

Giving Faces to the Lost

tual person, but it needs to look enough like the victim that a friend, family member, coworker, or acquaintance will recognize it. Creating a realistic and accurate reconstruction takes a lot of talent and care on the part of the forensic artist.

When all of the flesh has been added to the face, the artist adds as many details as possible to make it look realistic: color to the skin and lips; a wig, mustache, or beard; texture to the skin by blotting it with a damp sponge; eyebrows and eyelashes; wrinkles to an older person; or sometimes a bit of clothing. The artist wants to make the reconstruction recognizable without making too many guesses that might make it inaccurate.

With computer scanning, several pictures of the same face with different features can be made. Changing a detail like a different hairstyle, a mustache, an eye color, or even a hat or glasses may be enough to jog a memory and give the investigators a victim's name.

Forensics is a multidisciplinary field, meaning specialists from many related fields need to work together. Among these many specialists are forensic pathologists, forensic entomologists, mark and trace analysis experts, document experts, and fiber analysis specialists. They work together with the medical examiner and law officers to solve crimes. Forensic investigators must understand a wide range of disciplines and appreciate everyone's contributions in order to do their jobs most effectively. Cooperation is key for a successful investigation.

Sometimes the remains are of people who died accidentally or naturally, who committed suicide, or who died hundreds or even thousands of years ago. In these cases, identification and confirmation of manner of death or age of the remains will be enough to end the investigation. In most forensic anthropology investigations, though, the victim died violently and relatively recently at the hands of another person. Once a murder victim has been identified, it is time for investigators to look for a killer. To do this, they must reconstruct the crime.

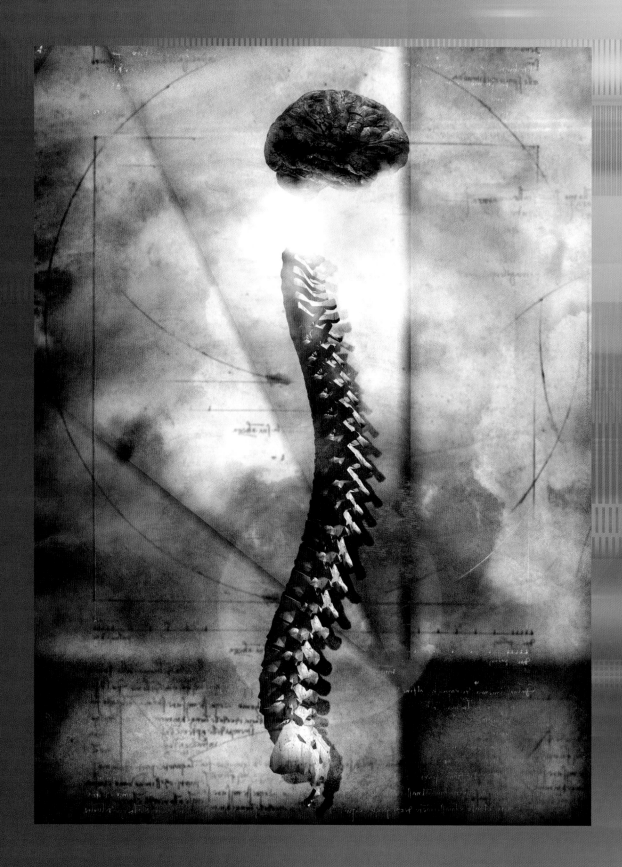

TAPHONOMY

In 1992, the city of Knoxville, Tennessee, was shocked by the Zoo Man murders. The bodies of four young women were found on a forest path near a major highway just outside of the city. The women had been tied and beaten, and three had been strangled to death.

Two of the bodies were in a state of advanced decomposition. The body of the fourth woman was so decomposed that it was impossible to recognize her face or search for any marks on her neck. The decomposition of her neck, however, was damning evidence in itself. Her face and neck were far more destroyed than the rest of her body. Called **differential decomposition**, this meant that there had been a wound—from her attacker's fingernails or another item—that broke the skin, making it an attractive place for flies to lay their eggs in the orifices of her face.

What could prove her manner of death? The **hyoid bone**. Unfortunately for investigators, it was missing from the skeleton. After returning to the scene of the

The Body Farm

Almost all we know today about the decomposition of bodies comes from the Anthropological Research Facility at the University of Tennessee—also known as "The Body Farm." Founded in 1980 by anthropologist Dr. Bill Bass, studies are carried out on donated bodies to investigate all the factors that affect decomposition. Bodies are allowed to decompose in sunlight, shade, buildings, vehicles, water, and all possible variables are tested to find important details that will help catch murderers and bring justice for victims.

crime and sifting bushels of soil, the crucial hyoid bone was finally found. It showed proof of breakage by strangulation; but the story was not over.

A suspect had been arrested. Known rapist and animal abuser Thomas Dee Huskey was taken into custody by the police, where he confessed to murdering the four women. However, this happened before the fresh-looking body was discovered. Overlooking the fact that the area was having a cold spell, keeping flies from laying their eggs on this body, defense attorneys argued that this woman might have been killed after Huskey was jailed.

Soil samples of fluid stains were taken from the area of the severely decomposed body to show **postmortem interval**. Studies were done on pig carcasses placed in the area to judge insect decomposition rates in the current cold temperatures, but all to no avail.

Unable to come to a conclusion, the jury was deadlocked, and the judge ordered a new trial. This trial barred Huskey's confession from being used as evidence, since in the midst of the confession he had asked for a lawyer, which he had not received. Huskey is currently serving a forty-four-year sentence for the rapes, robberies, and kidnappings of several other women, and may never be convicted of the murders of Patricia Anderson, Patricia Ann Johnson, Darlene Smith, and Susan Stone.

Forensic investigators must answer several questions to find a victim's killer. These questions are: *When* did a person die? *Where* did the person die? *How* was the person killed? *Who* did the killing? Taphonomy, the study of what happens to remains after death, helps answer these questions.

Decomposition

The rate of a body's decomposition helps forensic investigators most in determining when a victim was killed. Determining the postmortem interval can be crucial to identifying a killer. Rate of decomposition helps determine this interval.

Bodies decompose in a specific pattern. If the investigators can match this pattern to a timetable, they can tell when a person died. Several things affect the rate of decomposition. Heat and weather, indoor or outdoor location, insect and animal activity, clothing or other material, and placement of the body in a grave, into water, or leaving it exposed all affect the condition the body will be in when found. Each will help determine time of death.

All bodies go through changes after death. These are broken into two categories: early postmortem changes and decomposition. Early postmortem changes happen within forty-eight hours of death. How fast each change happens depends on the temperature and climate, size of the body, and whether the body is clothed or nude.

The first early postmortem change is called algor mortis, when the body cools. In algor mortis, the body temperature drops to the temperature of the surrounding environment. This will happen faster in a warm environment than in a cold one, and will happen faster to a nude body than to a clothed one. Forensic investigators will take this into account and use a mathematical formula to determine when the person died.

The next change is livor mortis, when the blood sinks to the body's lowest points. Wherever the blood pools, the skin develops a dark color, like a bruise. Wherever the body is actually touching the ground, or where blood movement is restricted, the skin will have a lighter mark. Anything lying underneath the corpse will also leave a mark or outline on the skin. Livor mortis is complete about two hours after death. After about six hours, the dark and light markings become permanent and will remain until the body reaches an advanced state of decomposition.

The third early postmortem change is rigor mortis. Beginning between ten minutes to three hours after death, the muscles stiffen due to lack of oxygen. Rigor mortis begins in the smallest muscles of the face and spreads throughout the body. This process can take up to twenty-four hours. After rigor mortis is complete, it will last around two days, until the processes of decomposition have gone to work breaking down the muscle.

Decomposition usually sets in within two days of death (although it can happen much faster in very hot, humid climates, or may be held off for years in frozen areas). Unless a body has been **embalmed** or mummified, the stages of decomposition will be the same. Six stages of decomposition follow the early postmortem changes. These are: early postmortem decay, putrefaction, black putrefaction, butyric fermentation, dry decay, and skeletonization.

Early postmortem decay means the first changes that begin to break down a body. These are caused by **enzymes** and bacteria inside the body and insects outside the body. During our lives, our bodies are filled with enzymes and bacteria that help us perform our bodily processes like digestion, respiration, and elimination of wastes. Our cells and organs contain these enzymes and bacteria. When a person dies, the cells and organs stop receiving oxygen, nutrients, and repairs. They begin to break down, releasing the enzymes and bacteria into the body, which then go on a feeding frenzy, traveling throughout the body and breaking down tissues.

While the body is being ravaged from the inside, insects break down its outside. The insects most responsible for breaking down decaying bodies are flies and their offspring, maggots. These animals are called necrophages, meaning "eaters of the dead." They are known by several names, especially blowflies and flesh flies. They look like slightly larger versions of common houseflies, who may also arrive at the big fly picnic.

Flies are attracted to dead bodies within about three minutes. As long as there is a way for flies to enter the area where there is a corpse, the fe-

Illustration of livor mortis

male flies will quickly begin to lay their thousands of eggs on the body. If a body is in an area with limited insect access, like inside a closed building or down a mine-shaft, it will take longer for flies to find the body and, therefore, longer for maggots to appear. In cold weather, insects become less active, with flies unable to fly at temperatures under 50 degrees Fahrenheit (10 degrees Celsius). Paying attention to all the conditions surrounding a body will help forensic anthropologists make good judgments about time of death.

Maggots grow in three stages, called instars. By examining eggs, instars, **pupal casings**, and adult flies, investigators can judge how long a body

Maggots

was in a location. Scientists who study insects at crime scenes are called forensic entomologists. While forensic entomologists are the experts, forensic anthropologists usually take the samples of maggots and other corpse insects and usually know enough about insect behavior in decomposition to make accurate judgments.

A body in early postmortem decay is still recognizable as the individual person. Forensic anthropologists are called in at the next stage of decomposition—putrefaction—when the body can no longer be identified by sight alone.

Putrefaction is the decomposition of a body by internal and external bacteria and other microorganisms, and by continued insect activity. The bacterial action causes buildup of gasses within the body cavities. These gasses are what cause the noxious fumes of decay. As the gasses accumulate, the body bloats, sometimes to three times its size in life. This bloating will cause bursting of parts of the body. The outer layer of the skin sloughs off, as does the hair of the head in one piece, called the hair mat.

As the internal organs break down, they turn into a thick, black liquid called purge fluid, which flows out of the burst areas and orifices of the body. At the same time, flies and maggots continue to feed on the rotting flesh. Flies seek out dark, wet places to lay their eggs, especially the orifices of the face, open wounds, genital openings, and the anus. These areas will be consumed first. As the body putrefies, the flies are joined by other insects such as ants, wasps, and some beetles, who feed off both the body and the maggots.

Putrefaction is followed by black putrefaction. This happens when the body collapses from the release of the built-up gasses and from the feeding of insects. The remaining flesh turns dark black and continues to give off noxious fumes from the activity of bacteria. At this point there will be a thick, greasy, black stain where the body was resting, caused by the release of purge fluid. Any plants underneath and immediately around the body will have died. Most of the maggots will have crawled to drier ground to pupate into flies. Though there may still be many maggots at this point, species of necrophagous beetles and their larva are the most common insects found on the body.

After most of the flesh has been decomposed by putrefaction, butyric fermentation sets in. The remaining tissue material ferments and dries onto the bones. Flies will have ceased feeding on the remains, and certain species of beetles will be the only remaining insects.

Meanwhile, if the body is in the presence of moisture and certain other substances called bases, saponification will have made adipocere form. Adipocere is a thick, greasy, white substance formed when fat decays in the presence of water and a base like lye. This greasy substance clings to the bones and the surrounding area, and can last many decades after a person's death.

Skeletonization means that the soft tissues have been consumed by bacteria and insects, leaving the bones and any remaining cartilage and ligaments exposed. A body can be partially or fully skeletonized. If the skeletonization is partial, the forensic anthropologist will usually have to clean the bones by boiling them in soapy water in order to further investigate the remains.

The age of a skeleton since decomposition can sometimes be judged by sight. Fresher bones are usually a brown color. Exposed bones bleach white over time. Bones also are luminescent, which means they will glow white under certain types of ultraviolet light. This luminescence is very strong in new bones and fades over time from the surface in. A new bone will luminesce strongly through its entire mass. As a bone grows older, the luminescence will fade, so an older bone may luminesce only at its core. An extremely old bone will not glow at all. It often takes hundreds of years

What Smells in Here?

Anyone who has ever encountered a road-killed animal knows that rotting corpses smell bad. But will someone always notice when a body is nearby? A skeleton in a vacant city lot, near two apartment buildings and a sidewalk, made police ask Dr. Bill Bass of the Body Farm that question. To come up with an answer, he gave students extra credit to come out to the facility and sniff around corpses. Careful records were kept of the distance between student and corpse when they first noticed the smell. The answer? The average person cannot smell a rotting corpse from more than thirty yards (27 meters) away.

for a bone to completely lose its luminescence, so this technique can be useful. Denser bones will keep their luminescence longer, which is important to keep in mind since some bones are denser than others; for example, Negroid bones are denser compared to Mongoloid bones, and young adult bones compared to elderly bones.

Mummification

Bodies are sometimes preserved by environmental conditions. When a body escapes decomposition because of environmental conditions, that body is said to be mummified. Most people are familiar with mummies produced by embalming processes, such as the ancient Egyptian mummies. These

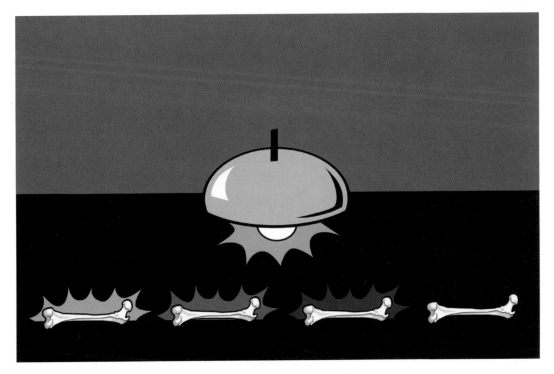

Illustration of luminescing bone

are not the only mummies. Bodies can be naturally mummified by extremes of temperature, lack of air, and natural chemical actions.

Extreme heat and extreme cold can lead to mummification. The key is low humidity. To mummify, a body must have all moisture in and around it removed as quickly as possible. Hot, dry deserts preserve bodies by quickly evaporating the body's moisture, drying the tissues and protecting them from bacteria and insects. Many mummies are found on cold, dry mountaintops, where moisture is wicked away by the air, causing the bodies to freeze-dry. These natural mummies will begin to decay if they are subjected to damp conditions or thawed.

Mummies are sometimes found in unexpected places where they formed because they were kept away from moisture and insects. These types of mummies have been found in the trunks of cars, in wooden or metal chests in houses, and in deep, narrow spaces like chimneys and mineshafts.

Sometimes very old bodies are found well preserved and fresh-looking because they've been kept in an airtight place. These bodies were often legitimately buried and then accidentally unearthed, dug up by grave robbers, or exhumed to be studied or relocated. Bodies buried in North America and Europe in the late nineteenth century (when embalming was becoming popular for the upper classes), sealed in metal coffins, and buried in clay soils (which have very little air between the particles) are the most likely to be found in this condition.

Natural chemical reactions in the area surrounding a body can also cause mummification. A famous example of this is the bog bodies found in northern Europe. These ancient bodies were preserved by peat bogs. The acids in the peat preserved the skins and soft tissues but softened and dissolved the bones. Gradually, layer after layer of peat trapped these bodies in the bogs, protecting them from air, insects, and scavengers. Two thousand years later, these bodies—probably the remains of human sacrifices—have been unearthed by people cutting the peat into blocks for fuel or for sale to gardeners.

Some murderers who try to destroy bodies are actually responsible for mummification. This is because many people believe that a mineral called lime, made from ground limestone, will dissolve a dead body. In fact, in the presence of moisture, lime will form a crusty shell around the body, protecting it from bacteria and insects and preserving it for investigators.

Bodies Found in Water

The presence of water also affects decomposition. Often, bodies retrieved from water are better preserved than those found on dry land. One reason is that flies cannot land on a sunken body, so insect activity is slowed. Water is often cooler than the surrounding land, and it protects the body from air and soil-borne microorganisms, so bacterial action is also slowed.

Another way that water preserves bodies is through the formation of adipocere. When the body is completely surrounded by water, adipocere will form swiftly and in large amounts wherever fats were present. This will preserve the bones as well as the shape of the body.

The one factor that makes bodies decompose faster in water than on land is scavengers. While most fish will not feed on a large corpse, a few will. Saltwater sharks and freshwater piranha are known for their attraction to the scent of blood, and they will feed on fresh corpses. Some bottom-feeding scavengers—including many species of crab—will feed on decaying corpses. The sea louse is another scavenging crustacean that will eat corpses. These tiny animals can swarm by the thousands and will sometimes strip flesh from a skeleton within a few hours.

Scavengers on Land

Bodies found on dry land are also vulnerable to scavenger animals. Not just insects but larger animals may carry off and consume parts of a body. This can pose a problem when investigators are trying to collect all the scattered bones of a skeleton. Knowledge of animal tracks, bite marks, and behavior will help the forensic anthropologist re-create the crime scene and recover the body.

Bodies left in the open or buried in shallow graves are the most likely to be preyed on by scavengers. Different animals carry off different body parts at different times, and for different purposes.

Birds and rodents can carry off a victim's hair to build nests. In order to recover the hair (which could help in identification) and to judge when

Arsenic and Death

Embalming first became popular in North America and Europe in the late 1800s. Morticians embalmed the bodies of wealthy patrons or of famous people by soaking them in arsenic, an extremely deadly poison. The practice was outlawed in the twentieth century. Several of these mummies were of famous outlaws, preserved so that their keepers could charge admission to see them. At least one, known as "Sylvester, the cowboy mummy," remains on display in Seattle, Washington. While most mummies are dry or frozen, arsenic mummies retain a wet, waxy appearance due to the effects of the poison.

the body was abandoned, the forensic anthropologist needs to know what types of birds or rodents would do this, what time of year they would be building nests, what the nests look like, and where they would build them.

Different types of animals eat different parts of the body during different periods of decay. A small predator, such as a fox, would eat soft parts of the body—the face, genital region, or areas around open wounds—during the early postmortem period and the early stages of decay. **Carrion birds**, like crows and vultures, are attracted to bodies in the early postmortem period and during decomposition. Rodent teeth marks are often seen on bones and usually occur after the body has reached the stage of dry decay. Rodents may also carry away small bones, such as the finger bones. Larger animals, like dogs, are attracted to bodies in states of smelly decomposition, and that is when they will carry off the larger bones.

Knowledge of animal behavior helps forensic anthropologists recover bones. Animals drag bones away from bodies in particular patterns. Investigators can chart where bones are most likely to be found, starting at the point where the body was originally placed. The original area can be found by the purge fluid stain and dead vegetation, which over time will be surrounded by new growths of especially healthy, well-fertilized plants. If the body was buried in a shallow grave, investigators will look for the disturbed area of soil and vegetation where the grave was dug.

As the search for bones continues, investigators must take into account the types of animals in the area. Coyotes may drag bones miles from the original site, whereas dogs will carry remains to nearby areas where they feel secure from surprise or attack to consume them in safety. Mountain lions often carry their prey into trees or cover them with branches; alligators may drag them under water, while large birds will rip off smaller pieces to eat at the location or to carry away. Tiny scavengers and predators, like mice and rats, will carry the smallest pieces to their food stashes or their nests, which will often radiate away from the body in a spiral pattern. Some herbivores, like deer, will even pick up long bones to gnaw and carry them away.

Knowing what the animal trails look like and where they are located is also helpful. Knowledge of animal prints helps with this. Often, these trails can be followed to scattered remains, including teeth and small bones found in the animals' waste.

Environmental conditions, like weather and running water, can also scatter bones. Forensic investigators must be very aware of their surroundings and of conditions where remains are found. This awareness will help investigators piece together the body, its identity, and the story of that person's death.

Carrion birds

Whenever remains are found in an area with leaf litter or soil, the soil around, near, and underneath the body (and the area where the body was originally placed) must be carefully sifted to recover all remains and all clues to the person's identity and death. This is a difficult, time-consuming task but very important in solving crimes.

Asking Where

As the forensic anthropologist figures out when a person died, she also needs to determine where the death occurred. These two questions go together. The forensic anthropologist examines the body and the surrounding scene to determine if it is the location of death, and if it is not, where that might have been.

Every bit of evidence must be recorded. Before investigators pick up remains, each piece is marked with a tiny flag so the pattern can be recorded. The position of the body is noted carefully. The forensic anthropologist must understand body movement. Did the body fall in a natural position, or was it moved after death? If the victim was found in a burned building, was she dead or alive when the fire started? Was he free, or was he tied or otherwise restrained?

Investigators sweeping a field for evidence

The forensic anthropologist must be able to tell if the body was left where it was found or moved from another place. Is there a purge fluid stain? Disturbed vegetation? A track where the body was dragged across the ground? Are bones or teeth missing? Sometimes the body will have marks showing that it was resting on top of something. These marks can be matched to its original location. After the entire body is accounted for as best as possible, recovery of the remains begins.

Unearthing remains is a very delicate process. Forensic investigators use archaeological techniques to remove human remains from crime scenes to make sure the remains are not damaged and that even the tiniest pieces of evidence are not lost. Using small, gentle instruments, like paintbrushes and garden trowels, the forensic team must carefully remove the body from the surrounding area. As the soil is removed, it is sifted through fine-mesh screens. Anything related to the body must be saved. Tiny fibers, dirt, a seed stuck to clothing, hairs—any of these might be the essential clue in identifying a victim or solving a murder case. Small bones, personal belongings, teeth, and bullets are especially likely to fall away from the body, so the sifting must be done very carefully.

Samples of the surrounding soil should be taken, as well as samples of insects on and near the corpse and of their pupal casings. Signs of violent struggle—like bullet holes, knife marks, marks from dragging a body, blood trails, and any other damage to surrounding items—must be recorded. Track marks from shoes or vehicles are photographed. If possible, fingerprints from the victim and the surroundings are taken. Anything that might contain DNA or other marks (like bitemarks) of the victim or the murderer—cigarette butts, partially eaten food, hairs, licked envelopes or stamps—is also collected.

An investigator unearthing remains

With the remains and the evidence, forensic anthropologists do their best to identify the victim. As the victim is identified, the forensic anthropologists must also determine from the body how the victim died. The answers to both these questions hopefully will help to catch the killer.

5

MANNER
OF DEATH

Two hikers in the Alps, along the border between Austria and Italy, stumbled upon a body on September 19, 1991. Thinking they had found the remains of a lost hiker or possibly a murder victim, they contacted authorities. It soon became apparent that this was not the victim of a recent accident or crime.

Named Ötzi for the region where he was found, this man died about 5,300 years ago. The glacial ice that trapped him made him the oldest complete mummy known. While freeze-dried and shriveled-looking, the cold prevented decay so well that his eyeballs are still intact. A facial reconstruction has even been done, showing what he probably looked like.

The hikers did turn out to be right, though: Ötzi was murdered. X-rays show that a slate arrowhead is embedded about 2.5 inches (6 centimeters) into his left shoulder, where it lodged after cutting through nerves and blood vessels,

Eyes and Decay

As a body decomposes, the eyes are usually among the first features to disappear. This is in part because they are very soft and attractive to scavenging animals. Birds are likely to consume the eyes and other soft parts of a corpse left in the open. Flies will choose the eyes and other body openings first to lay their eggs.

Another factor that causes the disappearance of the eyes is their chemical composition. Eyeballs have a very large amount of lysozyme, a substance produced by cells to digest organic materials. In a living body, the eyes' lysozyme digests things like bacteria that could cause damage. In a dead body, nothing keeps these enzymes in check, and like the other enzymes and bacteria in the body, they break down the body's own tissues.

Preserved eyes are very rare, even in mummified bodies, as the process of mummification usually dries all the tissues, or the chemicals involved eat away at the eyes' delicate structure. Ötzi's eyeballs are unusual because, instead of being destroyed or dried, the ice under which he was buried kept them soft and preserved.

paralyzing his arm. Ötzi probably died of blood loss and exposure within ten hours of being shot.

Since 1991, everything about Ötzi—his body, stomach contents, tattoos, clothes, and tools—has been studied. We will probably never know who

Ötzi was or why he was shot, but thanks to him, we know much more about how he and many of our ancestors lived.

Broken Bones

Most violent deaths leave marks on the victim's bones. To identify these marks, forensic anthropologists must know how to tell the difference between antemortem, perimortem, and postmortem injuries.

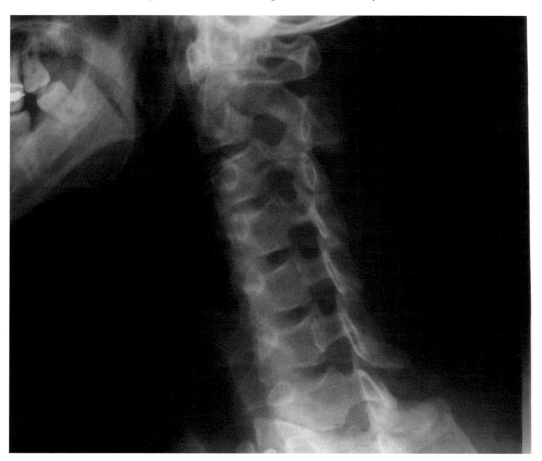

A forensic anthropologist will examine injuries to determine whether they occurred in the antemortem, perimortem, or postmortem period.

Antemortem means before death. An antemortem bone injury will show signs of healing. Our bones are living tissue; as a bone heals, it grows and changes. When a bone is broken, the body forms a **hematoma** around the break. The hematoma forms clots, and the bone grows a fibrous tissue around these clots. This tissue is called a callus. The callus grows and hardens, becoming a new growth of bone that holds the broken bone together. Bones take a long time to heal, and a skilled **osteologist** can tell how old an injury is based on callus growth.

Perimortem means at the time of death. These are the injuries that killed the victim or that happened while the victim was being killed. Perimortem injuries have had no time to heal. Living bone does not break cleanly; instead, it tears, twists, and splinters, like a green branch. If bones are broken in this way, the forensic anthropologist can be sure they happened around the time of death.

Postmortem means after death. Dead bones break cleanly, like dry branches. Attempts to destroy remains, scavenging animals, and environmental conditions can break bones this way.

To examine wounds on bones, they are first cleaned by boiling them in soapy water to remove any remaining tissue. They are then dried, laid out in anatomical order, and carefully examined for marks and injuries.

Although it is important to forensic anthropologists to help solve crimes, they work for neither the prosecutors nor the defendants in criminal cases. Forensic researchers work for the jurisdiction in which a crime is being investigated. Their job is to examine the evidence to the best of their abilities and present that evidence in an objective and unbiased way to a court of law.

When a forensic anthropologist finds perimortem injuries, he needs to determine what type of weapon caused the injury. Types of perimortem bone injury include bullet wounds, blunt-force trauma, sharp-force trauma, and strangulation breakage.

Bullet Wounds

Bullet wounds to the skull are the easiest to identify. Marks characteristic of bullet wounds are beveling, radiate fractures, and powder stains. The types of marks left by a gunshot depend on the type of weapon, the distance between the victim and the gun, and the direction from which the bullet came.

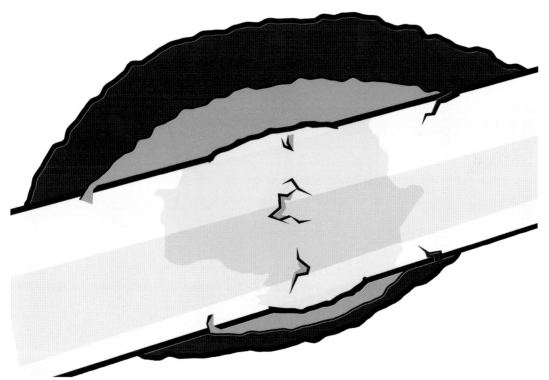

A bone that was broken in the antemortem period will have a callus and other signs of healing.

Beveling means that the wound will be smaller on one side of the bone than on the other side. Bullets always leave an entry wound and sometimes leave an exit wound. Entry wounds are beveled inward (larger in the direction the bullet was traveling), while exit wounds are beveled outward. If the bullet wound was to the skull and there is no exit wound, the forensic anthropologist will look for the bullet inside the skull. Missing bullets can also be found when the soil around a body is sifted. Shotgun pellets usually remain in a body and can be found by body X-rays.

Radiate fractures are cracks in the bone that radiate outward from the entry wound. If only pieces of the skull are available, the forensic anthro-

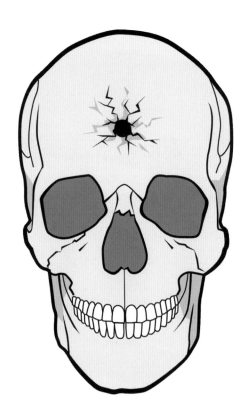

A bullet wound causes radiate fractures.

pologist can examine the direction of the fractures to determine where the bullet entered. Radiate fractures can also be caused by high-power weapons, because the speed of the bullet causes rapid buildup of gas inside the skull as the fluids around the brain evaporate. This gas buildup can crack the skull from the inside.

Powder stains are left on the bone around entry wounds when a gun barrel was in contact with its target. They can be burn marks from ignited powder or dark stains from unburned powder.

Gunshot wounds also leave marks on other bones of the body. These can be shattered bones, fractures, chips, indentations, or shotgun pellets lodged in bone. The pattern of fractures left in the skull is not the same as marks left on other bones, so forensic anthropologists must very carefully examine all bones, take careful note of all damage, and look for evidence of weapons in and around the body.

Stab Wounds and Sharp-Force Trauma

All weapons and tools used as weapons leave distinct marks. These marks can tell an investigator what type of weapon was used, the direction from which it came, the amount of force used to wield it, whether it was held in the attacker's right or left hand, and the order in which the wounds were made.

When most people think of knife wounds, they think of stab wounds. Actually, blades can leave several different types of wounds. Any wound left by a bladed tool is called sharp-force trauma. These tools include knives, chisels, pry bars, axes, hatchets, cleavers, and saws. Wound types include stabbing, slicing, slashing, hacking, cleaving, and dismemberment.

To determine the type of wound and the weapon that caused it, the forensic anthropologist examines the entrance of the wound, the sides, and the **furrow** or base. This examination can include viewing the wound under a microscope, which will show detail the naked eye might have missed.

Wounds are left by a weapon moving small pieces of tissue. Because bones are living tissue, they splinter as they break. A blade moving through bone causes the bone to splinter in the direction of movement. Looking at these splinters will tell the investigator the direction and angle from which the blade was coming.

Different types of blades leave different types of marks on the sides of wounds. These marks are tiny lines called striations. Think of cutting a piece of cheese with a serrated knife; you can see the striations clearly along the cut. The same thing happens with bones. An investigator can examine the striations and match them to a particular kind of weapon.

Stab wounds are created when a blade forcefully enters tissue from one direction and then usually is pulled back out. Slicing and slashing happen when a blade moves across tissue. Hacking and cleaving wounds are when a blade is brought down on tissue with a great deal of force. Dismemberment wounds are when enough force was used to separate a body part from the rest of the body. They are caused by hacking or cleaving weapons or by saws.

Saws are a huge subset of weapons used in dismemberment. There are dozens of different types of saws, each of which leave distinct marks on bones. Microscopes are often especially useful in examining saw cuts. Experts in dismemberment can match the type of mark with the type of saw used.

Blunt-Force Trauma

Like sharp-force trauma, blunt-force trauma can match wounds to weapons. Weapons without sharp points or blades cause these types of wounds. Unlike the hole left by a bullet or the cut left by a blade, blunt objects leave crater-like depressions with many fractures in the bone.

When a bone is hit with a blunt object, the area hit collapses inward. The bone cracks in layers, with the outside sustaining more fractures, and bone farther from the impact sustaining fewer fractures. These fractures radiate out from the point of impact. As the side that was hit caves in, away from the weapon, the bone on the opposite side from the wound bulges outward. So if a person is hit in the front of the skull by a weapon, the back of the skull will bulge away from the blow.

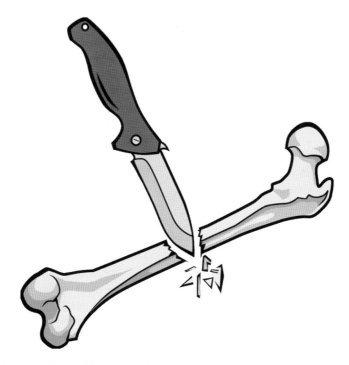

When hit with an object like a knife, bone will splinter in the direction of the blade's movement.

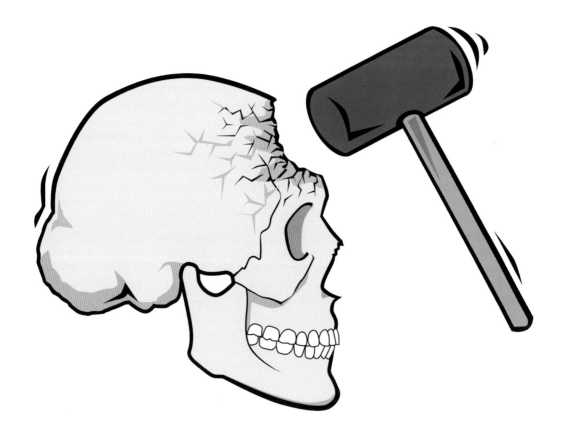

Blunt-force trauma causes crater-like depressions in bones.

Just like bladed objects, blunt objects each leave distinctive impressions. The marks left by a tire iron will be different from those left by a hammer, while different types of hammers also leave different marks. In both blunt- and sharp-force trauma cases, investigators also look for signs of individual tools, like chipped paint left in a wound or marks caused by imperfections in a blade or pounding surface. Hopefully, after a wound is identified, investigators will be able to match the wound to a specific weapon.

The Hyoid Bone

One small bone that can cause a big breakthrough in a murder case is the hyoid bone. The hyoid bone is located in the neck, below the chin. It is small, delicate, and almost always fractures in cases of strangulation. It will sometimes escape damage if the victim was a child, as children's bones are more flexible than adult bones. However, in most cases, at least one of the stems of the hyoid bone (which looks a little bit like a flattened chicken wishbone) will break when there is trauma to the throat.

Bone Fractures and Child Abuse

Several types of skeletal damage are particular to children who have suffered **chronic** abuse. These are multiple fractures, bone damage with gradient of healing, bone lesions, Harris lines, and lines of Retzius. If a child's skeleton is found, a forensic anthropologist will examine the bones for these signs to tell if the child was murdered after a long period of abuse. If this is the case, the parents or other caregivers are probably the culprits.

Multiple fractures can be caused by a variety of abusive behaviors, including shaken child syndrome. Shaking small children can cause bruising and fractures on the head and chest bones and chipping of the bones at the joints. Spiral fractures are common on the long bones of abused children. These are caused by grabbing and twisting limbs. Since children's bones are elastic, multiple fractures are much more common than large breaks.

Bone bruises and lesions are other common injuries in abuse cases. These are caused by blows and abrasions. In abuse cases, many fractures, bruises, and lesions are found. Some are new, some are fully healed, and

Forensic Anthropology as a Career

Forensic anthropologists in the United States are board certified and often are on the staffs of medical examiners' offices. In Canada, they are anthropologists who specialize in forensics but do not work full time in the field. To be a forensic anthropologist, you must have a Bachelor of Science degree in an area of the physical sciences (biology, chemistry, anatomy, physiology, or anthropology) and a Master of Science degree, usually in human biology or anthropology, or have graduated from medical school. You will also need a Doctorate of Philosophy (Ph.D.) in forensic anthropology. Board certification requires at least three years of forensic anthropology field experience.

some are in the process of healing. This is a healing gradient—when various stages of healing are found on the bones of one individual. A healing gradient means that the child has been severely abused over a prolonged period of time.

Two more signs of prolonged abuse are Harris lines and lines of Retzius. Harris lines are found on the bones, and lines of Retzius are found on the teeth. These lines mark where bone growth was stopped. Bone and tooth growth can be interrupted by starvation, severe illness, and severe psychological stress. Sadly, many children who die of abuse have suffered all of these, so remains with these characteristics almost always indicate severe abuse leading to murder.

While forensic anthropologists are often called to investigate murders or accidents involving only one or a few victims, they are also needed at scenes of disasters, sometimes involving dozens, hundreds, or even thousands of victims. In these cases, skeletons are usually disarticulated, often fragmented, and the remains of many individuals may be mixed together and scattered over a large area that must be thoroughly excavated.

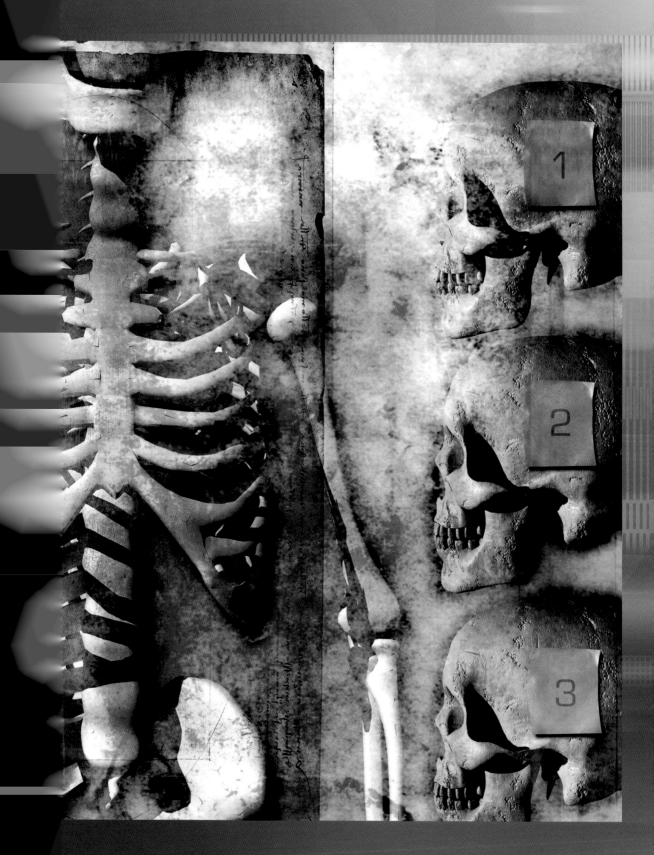

CHAPTER

6

BURNED AND MASS REMAINS

Forensic anthropologists often work on cases where bones have been damaged and are difficult to identify. Fire is a major force that damages remains and is often used by perpetrators trying to hide a crime. Luckily for investigators, fire does not destroy human remains.

Professional *cremations* need temperatures of at least 1,800 degrees Fahrenheit (982.2 degrees Celsius) for at least eighteen hours to reduce a human body to ash and bone fragments. Most house fires burn between 900 (482.2 degrees Celsius) and 1,800 degrees Fahrenheit for less than eight hours. Vehicle fires burn for an even shorter length of time. Even professional cremations often leave large enough bone fragments to identify a decedent, so arson fires rarely damage evidence enough to hinder an investigation.

The human body is composed mostly of water. Even bones are moist! To damage a skeleton, fire must first destroy all the soft tissues—including muscles, fat, and organs—that surround the bones. Rarely is a fire hot and long-lasting enough to fully destroy these soft tissues. Even if they are destroyed, most bone survives cremation, and forensic anthropologists can piece together nearly intact skeletons from burned remains.

How Fire Changes Bone

Bones go through different stages of damage by fire. They warp, fracture, fragment, and calcify. As a body begins to burn, all muscles and connective tissues, including ligaments and tendons, contract and twist. This pulls the limbs in toward the body as the torso and neck bend inward. This is called the pugilistic posture. A body in the pugilistic posture has its knees pulled up tightly, its arms pulled up in front of its face, and its hands curled into fists. If a burned body is found that is not in the *pugilistic* posture, it means that it was restrained during the burning (for example, the person was tied up), or that all of the flesh was removed before the fire.

As the soft tissues contract and twist, the bones warp and fracture. Warping means that the bones twist into different shapes as their moisture evaporates. Warping of the bone causes *longitudinal* fractures. Pressure from the contraction of the soft tissues causes horizontal fractures. A bone burned with flesh on it will have horizontal and longitudinal fractures. A bone burned without flesh will have only longitudinal fractures. A fourth-degree burn is when all tissues are burned off a skeleton. After the flesh has burned away, fire continues to change the bones.

The bones of the skull are often the first to fragment. This is because as the brain and cranial fluids boil, steam builds up inside the skull. The pressure of the steam makes the skull explode. As the fire continues, the bones lose moisture and organic materials, and they begin to shrink. The dense long bones may fragment into small, crescent-shaped pieces. Smaller bones of the arms and legs may break into square pieces. If the fire continues, the skeleton will become disarticulated, with the hands and feet breaking away first, followed by the arms, legs, and skull.

As bones burn, they calcify, meaning that all the organic materials are burned away, leaving only the minerals. As bones calcify, their color changes. Slightly damaged bones that still have their natural fats are yellow or brown. As the fats burn away, the bones **carbonize** and become black. As the carbon and all other organic materials burn away they turn gray, then blue-gray. Bones that are fully calcified are white. Teeth also carbonize, turning ash-gray. Calcified remains are extremely fragile. Fully calcified remains have basically been turned to ash and may crumble when touched. For this reason, extreme care must be taken with burned remains.

As with any crime or disaster scene, fire scenes must be carefully excavated. Forensic investigators must clear small areas at a time to get an idea

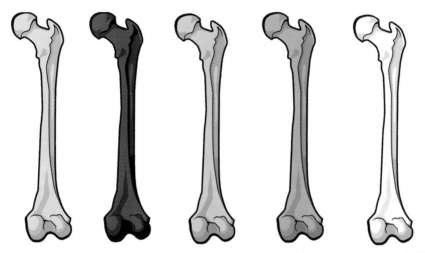

When burned, bone passes through a number of stages as it calcifies

Burned and Mass Remains　　**81**

of where the victims were during the fire and how the fire started. This will show whether the victims died before or during the fire, and if foul play was involved. It can also show if the bodies were moved and help identify the remains. Like soil at a crime scene, ash must be sifted to find identifying items, small bones and teeth, and other clues.

It is essential that investigators carefully photograph the entire scene and all remains before beginning recovery work. The forensic anthropologist must be allowed to investigate remains at the scene of the crime or other disaster. Huge amounts of evidence, including fragile remains that may be destroyed if they are moved, are available at the scene. Seeing remains in the context where they were found helps reconstruct events, identify victims, solve crimes, and piece together remains.

Mass Disasters

Airplane and train crashes, earthquakes and other natural disasters, and terrorist attacks are physically and emotionally difficult for recovery workers. They must work against time to recover and identify body parts before putrefaction makes this more difficult or impossible. In these types of disasters, dozens, hundreds, or even thousands of relatives and friends are waiting to know what became of their loved ones, adding to the workers' stress.

When these disasters happen in North America, DMORT, the Disaster Mortuary Operational Response Team, is usually called to assist. This is an organization formed by the United States Public Health Service. Volunteers from the forensics and mortuary fields work in the collection and identification of remains.

The procedure is the same whenever remains are fragmented and scattered. First, the area is studied carefully and small flags are placed to mark the location of each piece without removing it. After each remain is

Case Study: The Hinton Rail Collision

This collision of a passenger train and a freight train was one of the worst transit disasters in Canadian history. The crash occurred in Alberta's Rocky Mountains in February 1986, when the two trains were somehow allowed to move in opposite directions on the same track. The freight train, much heavier than the passenger train and loaded with toxic chemicals, crushed the cars as it came to rest on top of the passenger train. The fuel from both trains and the chemical cargo burst into flame. Some passengers pulled themselves out, but most were trapped in the wreckage.

As rescue workers attempted to put out the fire and free survivors, they soon saw that most of the fatalities were fragmented beyond recognition. Moreover, train companies do not keep passenger lists, so no one knew how many people were on board or their names.

Forensic anthropologists from the University of Alberta arrived on the scene to excavate the disaster site and identify remains. Families of people who might have been passengers were asked to provide information on their loved ones, as well as descriptions of personal effects and medical and dental records.

Despite the huge scope of the disaster, which yielded tens of thousands of bone fragments, the recovery effort was completed in only nine days. Unfortunately, investigation of some disasters and recovery of their victims can drag on for years. War is one such disaster.

flagged, the forensic anthropologist can study the overall picture, looking for patterns that might help locate other remains or solve the puzzle of what happened.

After flagging as many pieces as possible, they are collected and sealed in plastic bags. These bags are stored at the mortuary area in evidence freezers or sometimes freezer trucks, depending on the size of the disaster. Once at the mortuary area, forensic anthropologists and pathologists try to match the pieces to each other and to the people from whom they came. In large disasters, this is a race against time and decomposition, as remains continue to pour in from the disaster area.

War and Genocide

War is one of the most pervasive and devastating human tragedies. Forensic anthropology is important in war situations for the identification and *repatriation* of the dead. Many situations can arise after a war where identification is needed. Old battlefields may be unearthed, war dead may have been buried in mass graves, or remains of individual soldiers may go unidentified for decades. In each of these cases, eventually the bodies are exhumed, and all attempts are made to identify the deceased and to notify and return them to their countries and loved ones.

Genocide often goes hand in hand with war. Genocide is an attempt by one group of people to completely exterminate another group of people, including the mass murder of civilians. Incidences of genocide have happened throughout human history and are still happening in many areas of the world. The twentieth century alone saw the genocide of Jews and other ethnic minorities, like the **Romany**, in Hitler's concentration camps; the slaughter of millions of Cambodians by the military dictator Pol Pot; and the slaughter of hundreds of thousands to millions of unarmed civilians

Forensics Careers

Many exciting careers in forensics are available that require various levels of education. Criminalists work at crime scenes and crime labs and specialize in many areas, including fingerprints, weapon marks, crime-scene analysis, and evidence gathering. Crime-scene investigators collect evidence. Evidence custodians process and store it. Forensic investigators visit scenes, take custody of bodies, and collect possible evidence from the victims' families. Forensic pathologists are doctors who examine identifiable bodies. Forensic toxicologists specialize in identifying chemicals, including drugs. Forensic psychologists give insights into perpetrators' motives and thought processes. Document examiners, photo technicians, print examiners . . . all work together to make forensic investigations successful.

by military uprisings in Bosnia, Rwanda, and the Sudan. In many of these areas, the total number of the dead is still unknown. In other areas, people continue to live in fear of attacks and murder by armed militias. For many of these people, aid from the outside world will come too late.

Once genocide has happened, forensics investigators can still try to bring justice to the victims. When a mass burial is suspected, forensic techniques are used to survey the area. Archaeological techniques are used to dig into the area and to uncover any human remains. Once remains are uncovered, they are carefully reclaimed in the same manner as remains from mass disasters. Investigators attempt to identify the dead and the manner of death. Their goals are to build the case against the perpetrators and to return the remains to their families.

War is a terrible tragedy affecting the lives of everyone involved. When a family's son or daughter is killed in combat it is devastating to those left behind. The effect can be even worse when the person is missing in action, and the family has no certain knowledge of what became of their loved one. This is why most armed forces have a policy of recovery and repatriation for their members. This means that when a member of the armed forces is killed in the line of duty, every attempt will be made to recover the remains and to return them to their country and family for proper funeral services.

In these cases, it does not matter if the person was killed ten days ago or one hundred years ago. The United State continues its efforts to reclaim the remains of its missing service-people from as long ago as World War II and the Vietnam War. Even when the hidden remains of U.S. Civil War dead are occasionally unearthed, attempts are made to identify them and return them to their descendants.

Mass Burials and the Disappeared

Sometimes mass burials are found that are not directly related to a war. These are often cases where a government kills people it finds threatening. These people are known as "the disappeared" because they are usually kidnapped from their homes, taken to parts unknown, and never heard from again. Under these regimes, people have lived in fear, and family and acquaintances often have strong suspicions about what happened. In some of these countries, families stage movements asking for the end of the re-

Case Study:
Rwanda's Bones

One of the worst massacres of the twentieth century occurred in 1994. In Rwanda, as the world stood by, armed militias and rioters of the Hutu ethnic group slaughtered over 900,000 members of the Tutsi ethnic group in just one hundred days. Entire families and towns were slaughtered. Men, women, children, babies, and the elderly—no one was spared. The dead were buried in mass graves.

In late 1995, the United Nations Assistance Mission to Rwanda began attempts to exhume and identify the dead. Military personnel, archaeologists and anthropologists, aid workers, and doctors from around the world began the search for bodies and for identities.

Medical and dental records usually do not exist in such a poor nation. DNA testing was not possible because entire families had been slaughtered. Identification attempts were made by displaying the clothes and other personal items that had been found with the bodies. Since the slaughter was so extensive, in many cases no one was left to identify the victims. The effort continues.

Tomb of the Unknown Soldier

In Arlington National Cemetery, a simple monument honors soldiers from World War I, World War II, and the Korean Conflict for whom identification has proven to be impossible—so far. In 1998, the remains of the Vietnam unknown soldier were exhumed when DNA tests were able to give him a name. The family of U.S. Air Force First Lieutenant Michael Joseph Blassie was able to take him home to St. Louis, Missouri, and bury him. Some wonder whether, with the advent of new identification technology, there will ever be another truly unknown soldier.

Here Rests,
In Honored Glory
An American Soldier
Known But to God

gimes, freedom for **political prisoners**, accountability of the perpetrators, and reclamation of their loved ones' remains. Many of these regimes have already toppled. These include the Soviet Union and the military regime of Augusto Pinochet in Chile. Unfortunately, for every regime that has ended, several continue to exist, particularly in Latin America and Eastern Europe.

Mass burials are rarely uncovered that are neither the work of genocide, war, nor oppressive regimes. While serial killers are very rare, ones who conceal the remains of most or all of their victims in a single area are even rarer. When captured, these people leave evidence and remains of huge proportions for forensic anthropologists, archaeologists, and other investigators to sift through in identifying victims and bringing a perpetrator to justice.

Forensic anthropologists specialize in identifying the remains and last moments of victims of violent crime. They are, however, anthropologists as well as crime investigators. Anthropologists are scientists who study human beings, and the human family is at least one million years old. Sometimes the investigation of much older bones, what happened to the people from whom they came, and what has become of their remains over time, is just as crucial as the investigation of recent ones.

Burned and Mass Remains

Case Study:
The Vancouver Pig Farmer

Hastings Street in Vancouver, British Columbia, is known for its population of heroin addicts. Often homeless, sick, and desperate, a large number of these addicts are women. Poor and at the mercy of their addictions, these women often support themselves by prostitution. Crime investigators are familiar with the vulnerability of poor, homeless, and addicted women working as prostitutes; they see them as the victims of violent crime every day. With few people to stand up for them and few who notice right away when they're gone, these women are often preyed upon.

This is exactly what happened to the thirty women whose remains have been found on Robert Pickton's pig farm in Port Coquitlam, a short distance outside Vancouver. Some law enforcement officers, as well as some of the women themselves and their families and friends, began noticing the disappearance of Hastings Street prostitutes in 1983. The disappearances continued to climb. Family complaints increased, and one police officer noticed the pattern and warned the department that a serial killer was on the loose. That officer was fired, and law enforcement continued to stand by. In 1999, officials began to investigate the possibility of a serial killer.

In February 2002, Robert Pickton was arrested after the remains of two of the missing women were discovered during a search of his property. Pickton had been investigated several times before for a variety of crimes and suspicious activity, including a case of attempted murder after he stabbed a Hastings Street prostitute. Over one hundred searchers began combing the Port Coquitlam property in June of 2002. By July, more than one hundred anthropologists and anthropology students from the University of Alberta had joined the search.

Robert Pickton was convicted of six counts of murder and sentenced to life in prison. Prosecutors stayed a further twenty counts of murder, though he likely committed even more than that. Sixty-three women who have disappeared from Hastings Street are his suspected victims, and investigators believe he may have begun his killing spree as far back as 1971.

ANCIENT TEACHERS

The mummy joined the family in 1937. He was found by accident in a cave near the Rio Grande, on the Texas-Mexico border. The rancher, being Native American himself, considered the 1,100-year-old man to be one of his own ancestors. He was given a place of honor in the family home—first in a guest room, then in a special shed built for him. In 1986, the rancher's son allowed the mummy to be examined by Karl Reinhard, one of the world's only experts in paleoparasitology, the study of ancient parasites. Reinhard had become interested in the mummy because of an unusual feature he thought was related to the man's death.

The mummy's abdominal wall had rotted away, exposing a hugely swollen and distended intestine. This is a symptom of infection by a **protozoan** parasite called *Trypanosoma cruzi*. The parasite is spread by insects in the Reduviidae family, sometimes called assassin bugs, kissing bugs, vinchuchas, or bedbugs. It causes Chagas Disease, a disease in Latin America that currently infects between eight and eleven million people.

The protozoa attack lymph nodes and then nerve and muscle cells. While it can take decades for a victim to become seriously ill, it eventually leads to paralysis of internal organs that causes heart attacks, paralysis of the esophagus, and paralysis of the large intestine, leading to inability to eliminate wastes and eventual blood poisoning and death when the intestine bursts.

The find of *T. cruzi* in this ancient body is helping modern scientists study how long this parasite has been around, and may help them figure out where it came from and how to fight it. The mummy's find has already led to a DNA test for T. cruzi, which can help diagnose Chagas Disease earlier.

Bioarchaeology

Bioarchaeology is the study of past populations. It examines remains and artifacts to determine how a group of people behaved; their culture, habits, health, and other population trends. Bioarchaeologists often examine entire cemeteries and other large groups of remains to study a historical period.

Skeletons and mummified bodies are very important in examining the human past because they can teach us much about how people lived. Wounds, diseases, healed injuries, diet and lifestyle, age and life expectancy, and ritual treatment of the dead—all of these are written on bones. Mummified bodies can give even more information as clothing, personal belongings, individual features like hair and eyes, lifestyle, and pathology clues like parasites and last meals can be preserved with them.

Mummies can teach us a great deal about ancient traditions, religions, and cultures.

Skeletal and ***fossilized*** remains from ancient humans, human ancestors, and ***proto-humans*** have been found all over the world. For the most part, mummified remains have been concentrated in just a few places. Since these bodies were usually preserved on purpose, they give us many clues to ancient cultures and beliefs as well as to lifestyles and pathology. Even when preservation was accidental, cause of death and objects found in and near the bodies can tell us a great deal about our ancestors.

Ancient Teachers **95**

One Word Is Worth a Thousand Mummies

Sometimes a mistake in understanding one little word can have huge consequences.

The Crusades—medieval wars waged by Christian Europeans to conquer Persian and Muslim countries—began around 1100 CE. During these wars, many Middle Eastern artifacts were brought back to Europe, many of which were Arabic texts. While translating one of these texts, scholars came upon a strange word: "mumiya," the Arabic word for bitumen—types of natural tar or asphalt occasionally found seeping from the ground over oil deposits. The text described this substance being used as medicine. The translators, however, knew that this mysterious mumiya came from the land of the mummies and that bitumen was sometimes used in mummification. Not to mention that mumiya sounded a lot like "mummy." Somehow, this led them to believe that mumiya was actually ground mummy—human remains—used as medicine. The consumption of bits of mummies became hugely fashionable and was believed to cure all types of illness and injuries.

The travel between Europe and the Middle East for the Crusades became a gateway for the theft and transport of mummies. Thousands of Egyptian mummies were destroyed this way (aside from what probably became of the people eating them!), with the last recorded incident being as late as 1905.

Mummies Around the World

Areas with large finds of mummies are Egypt, the coastal region of Chile, the Taklamakhan Desert of northwestern China, the mountaintops of the Andes, and the bogs of northern Europe.

Egypt is especially famous for its ancient mummies, the oldest dating from about 4,500 years ago. These people were carefully embalmed as a part of their religion, which believed that physical preservation was necessary for the afterlife. Hundreds of thousands of mummies have been unearthed, from the well-known pharaohs in their pyramids to cemeteries of thousands of ordinary citizens. While European collectors or researchers performing autopsies destroyed many mummies, many still exist and are still being discovered today. Many hundreds more remain in museums and private collections around the world.

The homeland of the ancient Chinchorro people is on the coast of Chile, near the Atacama Desert. While most people have learned about ancient Egyptian mummies, they don't know that the oldest mummies in the world are actually from Chile. The Chinchorro people are the first we know about who practiced mummification. Some of these mummies are over seven thousand years old. The Chinchorro lived on the Chilean coast until 1100 BCE, when they disappeared for still-unknown reasons. At the beginning, they only mummified the bodies of children, probably as a way to ease the grief of their parents. By about three thousand years later, they mummified all of their dead. These bodies were encased in painted clay suits, including masks, and were left on top of the ground in massive cemeteries facing out to sea.

Near the homeland of the Chinchorro is the Atacama Desert. One of the hottest, driest places on earth, this desert is filled with the ancient dead, many of them thousands of years old. Its conditions are perfect for natural

One Picture Is Worth a Thousand Mummies

As the European Renaissance began, painters experimented with all types of strange recipes in the search for new and vibrant colors of paint. One of these colors was Egyptian Brown, made of ground mummy. Its use was first recorded in 1598. Though it was reported to make a beautiful, translucent shade of brown, within a few years the paint would crack and fracture, ruining the painting. Nevertheless, this color was quite popular and was produced and sold under the names "Egyptian Brown" or simply "Mummy" until 1903.

mummification, so lost travelers and victims of accidents are preserved as well as bodies purposely buried there.

The Taklamakhan Desert, in the Xinjiang province of China, is also an incredibly inhospitable region of the world for living humans. Alternating incredible heat with incredible cold, it is one of the driest places on earth. It also has vast salt flats. A mysterious **nomadic** people created their cemeteries in these salt flats, where their dead were naturally preserved. These bodies are around three thousand years old. Though the first of these mummies to be found was unearthed in 1895, they were ignored until the 1970s, when hundreds were discovered during surveying for the building of railroads and pipelines. Their study began in earnest in 1988. What is so incredible about these mummies is that they are not Chinese but Caucasian—and they were in China at least nine hundred years before the first known contact between China and Europe. They are believed to have been traders, moving goods between China and the rest of Eurasia along China's Great Silk Road. Judging from their clothes and artifacts, they appear to have had a high standard of living. Their clothing is different from anything native to China and appears to be similar to Celtic clothing of the same period. DNA tests show they originated in northern Europe. Ancient Chinese writings have also come to light that describe these European strangers, including records by Buddhist monks of the traders' language. This ancient language was Tocharian, an extinct language related to English, German, Gaelic, French, Spanish, and Greek.

Mummies are often laid to rest in elaborate tombs. Perhaps none are more elaborate than Egypt's Great Pyramids.

Dating Systems and Their Meaning

You might be accustomed to seeing dates expressed with the abbreviations BC or AD, as in the year 1000 BC or the year AD 1900. For centuries, this dating system has been the most common in the Western world. However, since BC and AD are based on Christianity (BC stands for Before Christ and AD stands for *Anno Domini*, Latin for "in the year of our Lord"), many people now prefer to use abbreviations that people from all religions can be comfortable using. The abbreviations BCE (meaning Before Common Era) and CE (meaning Common Era) mark time in the same way (for example, 1000 BC is the same year as 1000 BCE, and AD 1900 is the same year as 1900 CE), but BCE and CE do not have the same religious overtones as BC and AD.

The last two groups of mummies are usually not purposely preserved bodies but the remains of human sacrifices. One group is the Inca child mummies of the Andes. Dozens of these mummies have been excavated. As far as we know, these were children who were given by their people to the mountains, who were considered protective deities. The children were thought to have died by intoxication (with grain beer) and exposure (to the cold, oxygen-depleted mountaintops). These extremely sacred sites had elaborate shrines built around them and were attended by priests. The dead children were thought not to have died as a normal person dies, but to have become sacred oracles for their people. They would intercede with the mountain deities on their peoples' behalf, and their words would be interpreted and passed to the people by their attending priests. While the ancient Inca practiced mummification widely, possibly as widely as did the ancient Egyptians, when Spanish conquerors invaded their homeland, they destroyed the mummies in an attempt to also destroy the Inca culture and dominate the people. They were mostly successful.

The bog bodies of northern Europe are the second group of accidentally preserved bodies, probably of human sacrifices. Peat bogs exist in many areas of northern Europe, from Ireland through the Netherlands. These bogs were sacred sites to the ancient people who lived near them. Beautiful and unearthly, the bogs are created by peat, a thick, acidic type of moss, growing in water. Rather than turning into swamps, the peat creates vast, green expanses of solid-looking earth that roll and toss when a person or animal steps onto them, interspersed with pools of water. As new generations of peat grow, the old ones compress into thick, heavy layers. The acids and other chemicals produced by the peat discourage the growth of microorganisms and other creatures, which discourages decomposition of animal tissues. Huge finds of ancient artifacts have been unearthed in these places, sacrifices to the deities who were thought to live in an underworld accessible through the bogs. These finds include priceless artifacts of ancient craftwork, some as lavish as golden chariots, to the simpler sacrifices of common people, like new sets of clothing and shoes. They also include human and animal bodies. These people died as long as 2,500 years ago.

The difference between these mummies and most preserved remains is the lack of bones. The acids in the bogs leach minerals out of bone so that it is softened and often severely damaged by the weight of the peat; bones are sometimes missing altogether. The skin and soft tissues, however, are tanned and preserved. Most of these people show signs of having suffered a *ritualistic* death involving three types of mortal wounds—bludgeoning, stabbing or cutting, and strangulation. They are sometimes nude, sometimes clothed, and often placed face down, looking into the bog's underworld. The stomachs of several have been found to contain blackened barley bread and mistletoe—a sacrificial meal mentioned in ancient writings from the area. Other bodies have been found lovingly placed together, their arms wrapped around each other, presumably for all eternity.

Whatever the true stories of these people's lives and deaths, the mysteries they represent are fascinating, and the things they can teach us about our ancestors and ourselves are priceless. However, we must never forget to treat human remains with respect.

What to Do if You Find a Body or Suspicious Remains

If you come upon what look like human remains, stay calm. Do not touch anything. Remember how important every tiny clue can be to investigators! Leave the area immediately in case the situation is still dangerous, but be careful to remember where you saw the remains. Take note of landmarks that will help you remember where you were. Inform a trustworthy adult, and make sure that the adult immediately contacts the police.

Ethics and the Study of Human Remains

As with the modern war dead, repatriation is an important issue for dealing with ancient remains. It used to be customary for ancient remains in North America to become the property of museums and private collectors. However, since the 1960s there has been a move toward greater cultural sensitivity and civil rights concerning the fate of Native American people and their remains and artifacts. This move has been due in large part to the **grassroots** efforts of North American **First Nations** people to gain full recognition and civil rights for themselves within the dominant culture.

Full recognition of human rights includes respect for a people's cultural artifacts and the remains of their ancestors. Since 1990, the collection of Native American skeletal remains by museums and private individuals is illegal in the United States. Thousands of these bodies were in collections as of 1990, but if the remains belong to members of a tribe that survives today, it is legally required that they be returned to their people for proper **funerary** treatment.

Although the study of ancient human remains helps us understand our ancestors and, through them, where we came from and where we may be going, we must always remember that these remains were once living, breathing human beings. They had families and friends, homes and work, likes and dislikes. They loved and laughed and suffered, just as we do now. They had beliefs and hopes, some of which involved the respectful treatment of their bodies and their loved ones' bodies after death. We must treat them as we would want to be treated.

Moreover, *all* the bones studied by forensic anthropologists once belonged to living people. The forensic anthropologist's role is to use her knowledge to discover the truth about how people lived and, ultimately, how they died. When one human being takes the life of another human being, that crime demands justice. The forensic anthropologist's job is to work impartially toward that justice. In this way, our knowledge is furthered, our ability to uncover the mysteries of crimes is extended, and, hopefully, our ability to prevent crime will grow to the point where one day, forensic investigations are not so desperately needed.

Glossary

adipocere: A waxy substance formed by the decay of animal fat in water.

arsenic: A poisonous chemical element.

autopsy: The medical examination of a dead body in order to determine the cause and circumstances of death.

carbonize: To turn something into carbon by partial burning, fossilization, or chemical treatment.

carrion birds: Birds that scavenge for their food.

chronic: A condition that lasts over a long period or that frequently recurs.

cranium: The skull.

cremations: The professional burning of dead bodies until only ashes remain.

CT-scan: Computed tomography; a technique for producing images of the cross-sections of a body.

decedent: A dead person.

deciduous teeth: Baby teeth, also called milk teeth.

dentition: The number, type, and arrangement of teeth, different for different species.

differential decomposition: The process in which parts of a body decompose at different rates.

disarticulated: Separated at the joints.

embalmed: Preserved a body by chemical means.

enzymes: Complex proteins produced by living cells that aid in the body's chemical processes.

exhumed: Dug up a buried body, usually to look for evidence of a crime.

First Nations: The Canadian term for the Native people of the Americas.

forensic odontologist: A dentist who specializes in criminal investigations.

fossilized: Preserved by the replacement of organic compounds with minerals.

funerary: Related to or suitable for a burial or funeral.

furrow: The point of a wound furthest from the weapon's entry site.

gracile: Smooth, light, or delicate.

grassroots: The ordinary people (nonleaders) in a community or the ordinary members of an organization.

hematoma: A mass of blood material gathered at site the of trauma.

herbivores: Animals that only eat grass and other plants.

humerus: The long bone of the human upper arm or in a forelimb in other animals.

hyoid bone: The bone located in the throat below the jawbone and usually broken in cases of strangulation.

longitudinal: Extending from the top to the bottom of something.

medical examiner: A physician who is usually appointed by a state or local government to establish the cause of someone's death.

nasal aperture: The nose opening in the skull.

nomadic: Characterized by moving from place to place, often seasonally.

ocular orbits: The eye openings in the skull.

oracles: People or things who are considered to be sources of knowledge, wisdom, or prophecy.

osteologist: Someone who studies the structure and function of bones.

pathologists: Doctors who specialize in the changes caused by disease in tissues and body fluids.

peat bogs: Areas of land composed primarily of peat, compacted, partially decomposed organic debris.

political prisoners: Persons imprisoned by governments for their beliefs or perceived beliefs, rather than for any crime.

polyurethane resin: A synthetic plastic.

postmortem interval: The length of time between death and corpse discovery.

potash: A potassium compound primarily used in fertilizer.

proto-humans: Early human-like primates.

protozoan: Having to do with single-cell organisms that can move and feed on organic compounds of nitrogen and carbon.

puberty: The stage of development in which one becomes physiologically capable of sexual reproduction.

pugilistic: Having the characteristics of a boxer.

pupal casings: "Shells" shed by insects as they transform from pupae into adults.

repatriation: The return of someone to their country or cultural group.

ritualistic: Part of a ritual, an established pattern of observance.

robust: Heavy, rough, or thick.

Romany: An ethnic minority, commonly called "gypsies," found primarily in Europe, Northern Africa, the Americas, and the Indian subcontinent.

saponification: The chemical reaction between body fats, water, and a base, resulting in adipocere.

sutures: Joints, found espec ially in the skull, in which the bones are bound tightly together so no movement can occur.

wicked: Removed liquid.

Further Reading

Bass, Bill, and Jon Jefferson. *Death's Acre: Inside the Legendary Forensic Lab—Where the Dead Do Tell Tales.* New York: G. P. Putnam's Sons, 2003.

Burenhult, Goran (ed.). *People of the Past: The Epic Story of Human Origins and Development.* San Francisco, Calif.: Fog City Press, 2003.

Cornwell, Patricia. *Portrait of a Killer: Jack the Ripper—Case Closed.* New York: G. P. Putnam's Sons, 2002.

Craig, Emily. *Teasing Secrets from the Dead.* New York: Crown Publishers, 2004.

Manhein, Mary H. *The Bone Lady: Life as a Forensic Anthropologist.* Baton Rouge: Louisiana State University Press, 1999.

Pringle, Heather. *The Mummy Congress: Science, Obsession, and the Everlasting Dead.* New York: Hyperion, 2001.

Rhine, Stanley. *Bone Voyage.* Albuquerque: University of New Mexico Press, 1998.

Ubelaker, Douglas, and Henry Scammell. *Bones: A Forensic Detective's Casebook.* New York: Harper Collins, 2000.

For More Information

American Academy of Forensic Sciences
www.aafs.org

Amnesty International Canada: Stolen Sisters:
Discrimination and Violence Against Indigenous Women in Canada
www.amnesty.ca/our-work/issues/indigenous-peoples/no-more-stolen-sisters

Bodies of Evidence
www.trutv.com/shows/body_of_evidence/index.html

Child Protection Sites, Canada
www.canlaw.com/rights/childsave.htm

Crime Library: True Crime Stories and Forensics Files
www.crimelibrary.com

Forensic Anthropology and Human Osteology Resources
www.forensicanthro.com

National Missing Children's Locate Center, United States
www.nmclc.org/

University of Tennessee Anthropology Department
web.utk.edu/~anthrop

Vancouver Missing: Dedicated to the Missing Women of Vancouver, British Columbia
missingpeople.net/home.html

Publisher's note:
The websites listed on this page were active at the time of publication. The publisher is not responsible for websites that have changed their addresses or discontinued operation since the date of publication. The publisher will review and update the website list upon each reprint.

Index

Picture Credits

Artville: p. 13

Benjamin Stewart: pp. 32, 50, 60, 62

BrandX Pictures: pp. 8, 16, 30, 44, 64, 78, 92

Corel: p. 95

Evangeline Ehl: pp. 23, 49, 54, 69, 70, 73, 74, 81

Photodisc: pp. 10, 14, 26

Photos.com: pp. 19, 20, 36, 59, 67, 99

Biographies

AUTHOR

Angela Libal is a writer living in Los Angeles, California. She received her B.A. from Sarah Lawrence College in 1998 and studied anthropology at Los Angeles Valley College. She is currently pursuing a degree in the biological sciences.

SERIES CONSULTANTS

Carla Miller Noziglia is Senior Forensic Advisor for the U.S. Department of Justice, International Criminal Investigative Training Assistant Program. A Fellow of the American Academy of Forensic Sciences, Ms. Noziglia served as chair of the board of Trustees of the Forensic Science Foundation. Her work has earned her many honors and commendations, including Distinguished Fellow from the American Academy of Forensic Sciences (2003) and the Paul L. Kirk Award from the American Academy of Forensic Sciences Criminalistics Section. Ms. Noziglia's publications include *The Real Crime Lab* (coeditor, 2005), *So You Want to be a Forensic Scientist* (coeditor, 2003), and contributions to *Drug Facilitated Sexual Assault* (2001), *Convicted by Juries, Exonerated by Science: Case Studies in the Use of DNA* (1996), and the *Journal of Police Science* (1989). She is on the editorial board of the *Journal for Forensic Identification*.

Jay Siegel is Director of the Forensic and Investigative Sciences Program at Indiana University-Purdue University, Indianapolis and Chair of the Department of Chemistry and Chemical Biology. He holds a Ph.D. in Analytical Chemistry from George Washington University. He worked for three years at the Virginia Bureau of Forensic Sciences, analyzing drugs, fire residues, and trace evidence. From 1980 to 2004 he was professor of forensic chemistry and director of the forensic science program at Michigan State University in the School of Criminal Justice. Dr. Siegel has testified over 200 times as an expert witness in twelve states, Federal Court and Military Court. He is editor in chief of the *Encyclopedia of Forensic Sciences*, author of *Forensic Science: A Beginner's Guide and Fundamentals of Forensic Science*, and he has more than thirty publications in forensic science journals. Dr. Siegel was awarded the 2005 Paul Kirk Award for lifetime achievement in forensic science. In February 2009, he was named Distinguished Fellow by the American Academy of Forensic Sciences.